# How to Deal
# with Stress

# THE SUNDAY TIMES

# How to Deal with Stress

**Stephen Palmer and Cary Cooper**
Second Edition

KoganPage

LONDON  PHILADELPHIA  NEW DELHI

*For Maggie who has supported me for over two decades. (SP)*
*To my children, Scott, Beth, Lauren and Sarah. (CC)*

**Publisher's note**
Every possible effort has been made to ensure that the information contained in this book is accurate at the time of going to press, and the publishers and authors cannot accept responsibility for any errors or omissions, however caused. No responsibility for loss or damage occasioned to any person acting, or refraining from action, as a result of the material in this publication can be accepted by the editor, the publisher or either of the authors.

First published in Great Britain and the United States in 2007 by Kogan Page Limited
Reprinted 2007, 2008
Second edition 2010

| 120 Pentonville Road | 525 South 4th Street, #241 | 4737/23 Ansari Road |
| London N1 9JN | Philadelphia PA 19147 | Daryaganj |
| United Kingdom | USA | New Delhi 110002 |
| www.koganpage.com | | India |

© Stephen Palmer and Cary Cooper, 2007, 2010

The right of Stephen Palmer and Cary Cooper to be identified as the authors of this work has been asserted by them in accordance with the Copyright, Designs and Patents Act 1988.

ISBN    978 0 7494 5619 1
E-ISBN  978 0 7494 5912 3

The views expressed in this book are those of the authors and not necessarily the same as those of Times Newspapers Ltd.

**British Library Cataloguing-in-Publication Data**

A CIP record for this book is available from the British Library.

**Library of Congress Cataloging-in-Publication Data**

Palmer, Stephen, 1955–
   How to deal with stress / Stephen Palmer, Cary Cooper, -- 2nd edn.
      p. cm.
   Includes bibliographical references.
   ISBN 978-0-7494-5619-1 ISBN 978-0-7494-5912-3   1. Stress management.   I. Cooper, Cary L.   II. Title.
   RA785.P344 2010
   616.9'8--dc22

                                                                2009043256

Typeset by Jean Cussons Typesetting, Diss, Norfolk
Printed and bound in India by Replika Press Pvt Ltd

# Contents

# Acknowledgements

We thank the Health and Safety Executive (HSE) for providing two case studies, the HSE Stress Indicator, The Stress Policy, Action Plan Templates and information relating to the Management Standards. These are reproduced under the terms of the Click-Use License. In particular, we thank Peter Kelly at the HSE for guidance relating to the Stress Indicator tool. The general stress questionnaires are reproduced from *Living with Stress* by C L Cooper, R D Cooper and L H Eaker, previously published by Penguin in 1988.

*Stephen Palmer*
*Cary Cooper*

# Introduction

- Feeling stressed?
- Procrastinating when you have important projects to complete?
- Generally irritable, snappy and easily angered?
- Having difficulty managing pressures?
- Make mountains out of molehills?
- Never seem to have enough time for work or play?
- Fed up with life?
- Beat yourself up over trivial mistakes?
- Suffering more from coughs, sore throats and colds recently?
- Generally act in a passive or aggressive manner?
- Unable to concentrate or stay focused on any important task whether large or small?
- Becoming forgetful?
- Low self-esteem or self-worth?
- Often anxious?
- Daydreaming instead of living in the present?

Do you recognise any of the above? If you do, then this book is just what you have been looking for to help you change your life. Unlike most books on dealing with stress, this one will explain exactly why you act in stress-inducing ways and make your life – and possibly others' – a misery at times.

Do you ever wonder why, as soon as you are given an important project or task to work on, you find yourself tidying up your office, home, computer files, watching daytime television or starting comfort eating? Why do you 'make mountains out of molehills', and how can you stop this unhelpful approach to mismanaging your levels of stress? Do you recognise those 'musts', 'oughts' and 'shoulds' you regularly use against yourself and others to add intolerable pressure and stress to life? How often are you in a situation where you say out loud, 'I can't stand it any more'? Yet there you are, living proof that you can stand it!

This book, written by two international stress experts, gives an in-depth insight into the causes of stress and how to successfully deal with them. What may surprise you is how much we are directly responsible for our own levels of stress at work and at home. The good news is that this puts the reader in an advantageous position of being able to reduce levels of stress if and when necessary.

The book is divided into nine chapters. Chapter 1 looks at what stress is and includes definitions, balancing pressure and stress, locus of control and the biology of stress. Chapter 2 provides a working model of stress that underpins the approach of the book, and looks at the importance of life events and the concept of helpful and unhelpful negative emotions. Chapter 3 takes a psychological approach to tackling stress, and provides many strategies for changing our stress-inducing and goal-blocking perceptions, attitudes, rules and beliefs. This will really help to take the trauma out of a crisis. There is no more need to make a mountain out of a molehill. This chapter also considers improving confidence, self-esteem and self-acceptance, which are aspects of stress.

Chapter 4 focuses on the images or pictures you may have which sometimes create high levels of stress and reduce performance. For example, if you become anxious about giving a presentation at work or to colleagues on a college course you are attending, you may have unhelpful negative images in your mind's eye. This chapter really focuses on modifying these pictures or visualisations. Incidentally, sports psychologists and coaches do exactly the same with top athletes and the research shows that it really works! Yes, you can improve your golf without even going down to the golf club.

Chapter 5 concentrates on modifying your unhelpful behaviour by improving your interpersonal and time-management skills, and teaching you not to overlook the importance of support networks. Essentially, instead of becoming aggressive or passive under stress you can learn how to become assertive. This chapter also provides an insight into overcoming procrastination by using psychology and not just the usual standard time-management methods, which may not work.

Chapter 6 focuses on physical health interventions such as exercise, nutrition and relaxation techniques. These interventions may seem simple but they can really help to build up resistance to help us cope with stressful periods of our lives, and the relaxation techniques can even reduce blood pressure.

Chapter 7 deals with work-related stress. Whether you are a manager, a supervisor or an employee, this chapter will help you to understand, recognise and take proactive action to manage or prevent work-related stress for you and hopefully your colleagues or staff. It includes a section on work-related stress risk assessment. Chapter 8 brings together the key stress questionnaire results from the previous chapters and gives you the opportunity to assess yourself. Finally, Chapter 9 helps to develop an action plan so we can become successful stress managers. It also helps you to assess whether you are a stress carrier, and whether you wish to become a life manager, too. At the back of the book there is a list of useful books, websites and organisations that work with stress management and prevention.

This book takes a self-coaching approach. We help you to recognise the possible symptoms of stress and to understand how we largely create stress for ourselves. Then we guide you through a number of stress-busting techniques, methods or strategies which you can then choose to use on yourself.

We should like to add an important caveat to this book. If you are suffering from undiagnosed physical or psychological symptoms, don't suffer in silence: consult your general practitioner (GP). If you attempt a stress-busting strategy from this book and find it unhelpful or anxiety-provoking, then don't use it. If you are suffering from very high levels of stress, we recommend that you seek help from an appropriately trained professional, such as your GP, psychologist or therapist (see the list of useful organisations at the end of the book).

This book could seriously help you to tackle stress and enhance your performance. Give it a go and join us on this journey!

# How to get the most out of this book

Most books are written so that the reader starts at the beginning and then reads through the text to the end. This book is different. Chapter 1 provides an introduction to the nature of stress, and Chapter 2 provides a working model of stress. After reading these chapters you can then dip into the remaining chapters if you so wish. Of course, our book has been written in a logical order so that to maximise your stress reduction programme, commencing at Chapter 1 and then reading the remaining chapters in order would be ideal, but it is not essential.

To understand, recognise and then tackle stress successfully needs some hard work and practice on your part. We can't do all the work for you! The chapters include questionnaires to aid understanding, activity exercises to put the techniques and skills we discuss into action to work for you, and at the end of each chapter a section for you to note down any stress-busting methods that you have found useful or wish to note for future reference.

In addition to using the book you may wish to note down useful stress-busting techniques on your computer or mobile telephone memo pad.

## Activity 1
## Your goals for reading this book

**Before you start your own personal stress management programme, it is important to consider what you are hoping to get out of reading this book. It may be to reduce stress, learn to stay relaxed at work, stop procrastinating over project work or studies. Just note down your goals and objectives below:**

**Goal 1:**

**Goal 2:**

**Goal 3:**

**Goal 4:**

**Goal 5:**

**Goal 6:**

When you finish reading each chapter of this book it is useful to return to your goal list above to help you to stay focused on your personal goals. Do revise it or add to it as you so wish. Remember, it is your own self-coaching programme.

One last point; if you are in coaching, your coach may recommend this book for background reading and may want to discuss the strategies and techniques with you. Our coachees have found time spent discussing and reflecting on their application of the techniques very useful.

# 1

# What is stress?

So what is stress? It is one of those terms that mean so many things to different people. For the purposes of this book, it may be a good idea if we have a common understanding. In this chapter we shall provide you with a definition of stress, highlight the difference between pressure and stress, and explain the biology of stress.

## Simple definition

There are many definitions of stress. The one we have found useful is:

Stress occurs when pressure exceeds your perceived ability to cope.

So it is not just external pressure, such as reaching deadlines, that triggers stress, but whether you believe that you can cope with a situation that you perceive as important or threatening. Obviously, the more experienced or skilled you are at a particular activity, such as giving presentations or completing projects on time, the less likely you are to become stressed.

But in many jobs there is constantly high pressure to perform, and no breathing space at all. Under pressure employees start working longer hours, taking work home, and in extreme cases work in their holidays to achieve work targets and deadlines. A time may come when, literally, the person passively accepts one project too many and then realises he or she just can't cope any more. We often hear the phrase, 'the straw that breaks the camel's back', but this is very relevant to the field of stress prevention, as we will highlight shortly.

Of course, if you do not perceive that the problem is important or threatening, then even if you do not successfully deal with it, you are unlikely to become stressed.

## Pressure and stress

To state the obvious, each person is uniquely different, for example in our genetic predispositions to suffer from various medical disorders, our hair colour, height, weight, level of fitness, personality, humour, interests and so on. This also applies to the amount of pressure each of us can take.

Research has shown that there is a real physiological difference between pressure and stress. People experiencing stress have higher levels of the various stress hormones in their bloodstream than people who feel merely challenged. At the right amount of pressure we work at our optimum. We will be effective, creative, decisive, alert and stimulated. We will start the day and look forward to our work, studies or other personal interests or hobbies. The important point to note is that this varies from person to person. One person's pressure is another person's stress. Too much pressure can lead to anxiety and burnout. Too little pressure, and we become bored, apathetic, depressed and finally may even reach rustout! The link between rustout, our optimum level and burnout is illustrated in Figure I.I.

In fact, when people are feeling appropriately challenged they often feel excited about accomplishing a task, whereas when they are stressed they usually experience a range of negative thoughts, feelings and physical sensations.

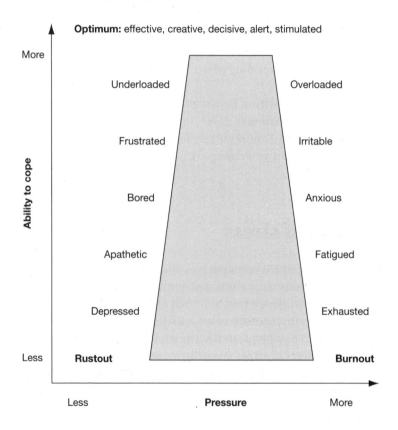

Source: adapted from Palmer and Strickland (1996)

**Figure 1.1**　The relationship of pressure to the ability to cope

The key to managing stress is to become skilled at balancing your workload and remaining in your personal optimal zone. However, first of all, we need to become more aware of how pressured we are during our average day or week.

## Activity 2

Reflect upon how you've felt in the past week and then think about the questions below:

- Have you been stressed, relaxed, bored or fatigued?
- Do you regularly work at your optimum?
- On your average day, where are you on the pressure diagram?
- Does your position on the diagram vary throughout the day or on particular days?
- Finally, if you are regularly feeling too much or too little pressure, can you change this situation, assuming you want to?

# Costs of stress

The costs of stress are immense. Surprisingly, stress has overtaken the common cold as a major reason for absence from work, and the Confederation of British Industry (CBI) has estimated that absenteeism costs British industry more than £10 billion a year. This is typical of many studies in the Western world. The effects of stress upon the individual are not encouraging, and studies have found it may be responsible for a variety of ailments, including:

- heart attack/strokes;
- hypertension/high blood pressure;
- ulcers;
- diabetes;
- angina;
- cancer;
- rheumatoid arthritis;
- psychological disorders such as anxiety and depression, including breakdowns.

To illustrate the effects of stress and why it is so important to tackle it as it arises, let's just examine a case study of a civil servant who kindly shares his experience with us (HSE, 2006a).

## Case study: Rehabilitation after an acute episode of work-related stress

I was brought up in an environment where the Protestant work ethic was very much to the fore. Success was largely measured by completing tasks – whether schoolwork, or household chores – that were given to me. This work ethic translated itself in adult life as a desire to work consistently hard and to a high standard, both in my Civil Service career, and in the voluntary work and academic studies I undertook in my spare time.

For 10 years I managed, through sheer willpower and hard work, to juggle the conflicting demands of a career in the Civil Service working on high-profile policy areas, and a variety of activities outside work. Occasionally the cracks would show, but I would paper over them, often by using holidays to complete work tasks.

Eventually, however, I could cope no more. The straw that broke the camel's back came one Sunday in February 1996 when a combination of factors, including a new, demanding job that I had taken on promotion and a difficult relationship in my personal life, resulted in my having a sudden and complete nervous breakdown. One day I was coping with a full and varied work and social life; the next I was incapable of undertaking even the simplest tasks. I retreated into myself and was only prepared to communicate with a handful of trusted friends and family.

Three painful and challenging months followed, with

spells in my local mental hospital. This period was made particularly difficult by the uncertainty about if and when I would ever recover, and by having to learn to engage with a bewildering number of different layers of bureaucracy. Linked to that was the question mark over whether I would ever resume my Civil Service career, and if not, how I would support myself financially.

Thankfully as spring gave way to summer I began to feel better. This was in no small part the result of the loving care and concern of my friends and family. By July 1996 I was in a position to consider a partial return to my Civil Service career. The thought of returning to work was daunting, not least the uncertainty over how my work colleagues would react following my extended absence due to mental ill-health. Fortunately the staff counselling service had enabled me to maintain indirect contact with my manager and my work colleagues. I preferred this indirect approach, as I was a little anxious about dealing with my colleagues directly at first.

Through home visits from the staff counsellor, I agreed with my manager a staggered return to work. Initially I worked two days per week. In my early days back in the office my manager had weekly meetings with me to check that I was coping with my workload in terms of both quality and quantity. In addition, other colleagues were incredibly supportive and understanding. This helped me to rebuild my fragile confidence in my ability to undertake my job.

After my first month back at work my manager subsequently reviewed my progress with me on a monthly basis. These monthly reviews resulted in my work pattern changing initially to three days per week, then four. Finally, by October I was ready to return to a five-day working week, although in contrast to before being ill I now had a much more realistic expectation of the amount of work I could undertake in a given period. I was also much more realistic about how much responsibility I should accept in my spare time.

Through this acute episode of work-related stress, I have learnt the hard way the importance of maintaining a healthy work–life balance. I know I have a tendency to work too hard, and can now spot the early warning signs of overwork and do something about it. Since 1996 I have also had the privilege to pass on what I have learnt to other people suffering mental ill-health as a result of work-related stress.

My staggered return to work demonstrates the value of active case management in ensuring successful rehabilitation. I was fortunate to have a competent and sensitive staff counsellor who was able to help maintain good communication between me and my workplace, and a manager prepared to be flexible in restructuring and reviewing my job to meet my changing needs. Things might have turned out very differently if I had not had a staff counsellor to use as a trusted intermediary in the rehabilitation process, and the local support network to encourage me to rebuild my life.

This case study demonstrates how our beliefs and attitudes that we take into the workplace can help to drive us on relentlessly. There are often alternative options or choices. For example, we can be assertive and inform our manager that we have been given too much work, too many deadlines and not enough time to complete the projects. Let's review the case study and see how our beliefs contribute to stress:

The Protestant work ethic was very much to the fore. Success was largely measured by completing tasks – whether schoolwork, or household chores – that were given to me.

However, once we become adults, if we reflect upon our beliefs we could challenge and modify them if we choose to. But most of us don't realise this, so we carry on with these beliefs and take them into college, university and the workplace:

> This work ethic translated itself in adult life as a desire to work consistently hard and to a high standard, both in my Civil Service career, and in the voluntary work and academic studies I undertook in my spare time.

High standards applied inflexibly can increase the demands and stress we place upon ourselves. This may work for a while, but for many of us it has repercussions. Pressured jobs and long hours can impact upon relationships at work and at home, and we can become emotionally and physically drained:

> I could cope no more. The straw that broke the camel's back came one Sunday in February 1996 when a combination of factors, including a new, demanding job that I had taken on promotion and a difficult relationship in my personal life, resulted in my having a sudden and complete nervous breakdown.

This person accepted a new demanding job, plus he had relationship difficulties external to work. This all became overwhelming and he could no longer cope. Fortunately, in our case study, he received support from his family and friends, and with the help of his counsellor he had a gradual reintroduction back into work. But he also learnt from the process and changed his previously unrealistic expectations:

> Finally, by October I was ready to return to a five-day working week, although in contrast to before being ill I now had a much more realistic expectation of the amount of work I could undertake in a given period. I was also much more realistic about how much responsibility I should accept in my spare time.

This was an important breakthrough. Sadly it took a nervous breakdown and subsequent help and support for this person to re-evaluate his previously strongly held beliefs, but this prepared him for his successful return to work.

To be realistic, our model of stress needs to take into account some of the factors raised by this case study. We return to it in the next section, where we introduce a model that helps to explain the link between our beliefs and stress. However, do note that in Chapter 7 we shall introduce a model that includes all the major organisational factors of stress too, and which gives managers an insight into how the organisation can help employees.

## How do you cope with stress?

Over time we all learn a number of strategies to help us deal with or avoid stress. Some of these strategies are adaptive and helpful, while others are less so. The next activity will help you to assess the effectiveness of your general approach to dealing with stress. It's worth noting down behaviours you need to do more or less of in order to tackle stress, as you do this activity.

## Activity 3
## Life Stress Questionnaire

Think of a personal stress-triggering problem. It could be a difficult issue to do with your partner, children, friends or family. Now consider to what extent you do the following below and circle your response to each question on the scale of 1 to 5.

**Table 1.1**

| Part 1 – Temporary adaptation | Never | Rarely | Periodically | Regularly | Very often |
|---|---|---|---|---|---|
| Get on with work, keep busy | 1 | 2 | 3 | 4 | 5 |
| Throw yourself into work | 1 | 2 | 3 | 4 | 5 |
| Do some housework | 1 | 2 | 3 | 4 | 5 |
| Attempt to do something where you don't use your mind | 1 | 2 | 3 | 4 | 5 |
| Cry on your own | 1 | 2 | 3 | 4 | 5 |
| Bottle it up for a time, then break down | 1 | 2 | 3 | 4 | 5 |
| Explosive, mostly temper, not tears | 1 | 2 | 3 | 4 | 5 |
| Treat yourself to something like clothes or a meal out | 1 | 2 | 3 | 4 | 5 |
| **Part 2 – Helpful behaviour** | | | | | |
| Sit and think | 1 | 2 | 3 | 4 | 5 |
| Ability to cry with friends | 1 | 2 | 3 | 4 | 5 |
| Get angry with people or things that are causing the problem | 1 | 2 | 3 | 4 | 5 |
| Let feelings out, talk to close friends | 1 | 2 | 3 | 4 | 5 |
| Talk things over with lots of friends | 1 | 2 | 3 | 4 | 5 |
| Go over the problem again and again in your mind to try to understand it | 1 | 2 | 3 | 4 | 5 |
| Feel you learn something from every distress | 1 | 2 | 3 | 4 | 5 |
| Talk to someone who could do something about the problem | 1 | 2 | 3 | 4 | 5 |
| Try to get sympathy and understanding from someone | 1 | 2 | 3 | 4 | 5 |

| Part 3 – Unhelpful behaviour | Never | Rarely | Periodically | Regularly | Very often |
|---|---|---|---|---|---|
| Try not to think about it | 5 | 4 | 3 | 2 | 1 |
| Go quiet | 5 | 4 | 3 | 2 | 1 |
| Go on as if nothing had happened | 5 | 4 | 3 | 2 | 1 |
| Keep feelings to yourself | 5 | 4 | 3 | 2 | 1 |
| Avoid being with people | 5 | 4 | 3 | 2 | 1 |
| Show a 'brave face' | 5 | 4 | 3 | 2 | 1 |
| Worry constantly | 5 | 4 | 3 | 2 | 1 |
| Lose sleep | 5 | 4 | 3 | 2 | 1 |
| Don't eat | 5 | 4 | 3 | 2 | 1 |
| Control tears (hide feelings) | 5 | 4 | 3 | 2 | 1 |
| Eat more | 5 | 4 | 3 | 2 | 1 |
| Wish you could change what happened | 5 | 4 | 3 | 2 | 1 |
| Have fantasies or wishes about how things might have turned out | 5 | 4 | 3 | 2 | 1 |

```
        Unhelpful                Helpful
        29          87           145
        |_____|_____|
```

To calculate your score, add up all the circled numbers and plot the total on the scale above. If you have a score less than *58*, many of your behaviours to deal with stress are not always very helpful, while a score of *116* or over would indicate that many of your behaviours are more helpful when dealing with stressful situations. On those items for which you have low scores, especially in Parts 2

and 3, consider how you might improve them. Do note
that the other chapters in this book may help you to
modify some of your behaviours and thoughts.

Source: adapted from Cooper *et al* (1988).

# Are you in control?

If you perceive yourself to be in control of a situation or life in
general, you will suffer from less stress, anxiety and depression
compared with others who do not see themselves in control.
Therefore control is seen by researchers as an important aspect of
the stress construct (Rotter, 1966; Ruiz-Bueno, 2000). The next
activity will help you to assess how much control you believe you
have over life in general.

# Activity 4
# Locus of Control Questionnaire

**Circle the number that best reflects your attitudes**

**Table 1.2**

|  | Strongly disagree | Disagree | Uncertain | Agree | Strongly agree |
|---|---|---|---|---|---|
| Our society is run by a few people with enormous power and there is not much the ordinary person can do about it. | 1 | 2 | 3 | 4 | 5 |
| Success is determined by being in the right place at the right time. | 1 | 2 | 3 | 4 | 5 |

| | Strongly disagree | Disagree | Uncertain | Agree | Strongly agree |
|---|---|---|---|---|---|
| There will always be industrial relations disputes no matter how hard people try to prevent them, or the extent to which they try to take an active role in union activities. | I | 2 | 3 | 4 | 5 |
| Politicians are inherently self-interested and inflexible. It is impossible to change the course of policies. | I | 2 | 3 | 4 | 5 |
| What happens in life is predestined. | I | 2 | 3 | 4 | 5 |
| People are inherently lazy, so there is no point in spending too much time in changing them. | I | 2 | 3 | 4 | 5 |
| I do not see a direct connection between the way and how hard I work and the assessments of my performance that others arrive at. | I | 2 | 3 | 4 | 5 |
| Leadership qualities are primarily inherited. | I | 2 | 3 | 4 | 5 |
| I am fairly certain that luck and chance play a crucial role in life. | I | 2 | 3 | 4 | 5 |
| Even though some people try to control events by taking part in political and social affairs, in reality most of us are subject to forces we can neither comprehend nor control. | I | 2 | 3 | 4 | 5 |

Plot your total score below

| Internal | | External |
|----------|----|----------|
| 10 | 30 | 50 |

A score of about 30 is average. A lower score is better, as you perceive you have more control over a range of different issues. You have an internal locus of control. A very low score may be unrealistic, so you may be surprised when unexpected life events occur that challenge your belief of almost total control. A score of over 30 means that you may have an external locus of control, and on a day-to-day basis may suffer from more stress.

If you have a high score of 40 or above, consider whether there are more areas of your life you could influence.

Source: Cooper *et al* (1988).

## Health locus of control

In addition to a general locus of control there is also a health locus of control. This focuses on our knowledge about health-related issues, and whether we perceive we can take action to influence our health. Instead of just asking the doctor, 'What can you do for me?', a person with an internal health locus of control is also likely to ask, 'What can I do for myself?' For example, you could choose to take a proactive approach to dealing with your obesity if you suffer from high blood pressure or raised levels of cholesterol, such as maintaining a healthy diet and taking more exercise. This could have a better long-term outcome than just taking medication that your doctor has prescribed for reduction of high blood pressure and raised cholesterol levels.

A caveat: do note that we are not advocating giving up prescribed medication. We are just suggesting that people with an internal health locus of control would ask the doctor, or find out elsewhere, what they could do to help themselves, in addition to taking the medication. Of course, we realise that their goal agreed by their doctor might be to reduce or stop taking their medication eventually.

## The biology of stress

As psychologists we occasionally meet managers or company directors who think that stress is 'all in the mind', whereas our stressed clients and coachees often tell us, 'I think I'm going mad.' Of course, how we perceive situations may trigger or exacerbate stress. However, once you are stressed a range of biological processes start in the brain and body which are very real. If you are fascinated by what happens, we have included a brief summary of the biology of stress in this section. Skip this section if you are keen just to learn how to fight stress.

Let's examine the stress response step by step (Palmer and Dryden, 1995):

- **When a person perceives he or she is in a threatening situation which he or she is unable to cope with, messages are carried along neurones from the cerebral cortex (where the thought processes occur in the brain) and the limbic system to the hypothalamus (located in the brain). The hypothalamus has a number of discrete parts.**
- **The anterior hypothalamus produces sympathetic arousal of the autonomic nervous system (ANS). The ANS is an automatic system that controls the heart, lungs, blood vessels, stomach and glands. Because of its action we do not need to make any conscious effort to regulate our breathing or heartbeat. It just happens without our thinking about it.**

- The ANS consists of two different systems, the sympathetic nervous system and the parasympathetic nervous system (PNS).
- The PNS conserves energy levels and aids relaxation. Assuming you are relaxed as you read this book, your PNS is functioning at this precise moment.
- The PNS increases bodily secretions such as saliva, tears, mucus and gastric acids, which help to defend the body and aid digestion. Therefore when you are feeling relaxed your immune system is working.
- The PNS sends its messages by a chemical known as a neurotransmitter, called acetylcholine. This chemical is stored at nerve endings.
- The sympathetic nervous system (SNS) prepares the body for action. This forms part of the 'fight or flight' response.
- In a stressful situation, it quickly does the following:
  - Increases the strength of skeletal muscles.
  - Increases the heart rate.
  - Increases mental activity and concentration.
  - Increases sugar and fat levels.
  - Reduces intestinal movement.
  - Inhibits tears and digestive secretions.
  - Relaxes the bladder.
  - Dilates pupils.
  - Increases perspiration.
  - Inhibits erections or vaginal lubrication.
  - Decreases blood-clotting time.
  - Constricts most blood vessels but dilates those in the heart/arm/leg muscles.
- The main sympathetic neurotransmitter is called noradrenaline, which is released at the nerve endings.
- The stress response also includes the activity of the adrenal, pituitary and thyroid glands.
- The two adrenal glands are located one on top of each kidney. The middle part of the adrenal gland is called

the adrenal medulla, and is connected to the SNS by nerves. Once the latter system is in action it instructs the adrenal medulla to produce adrenaline and noradrenaline (catecholamines), which are released into the blood supply.

- The adrenaline prepares the body for flight and the noradrenaline prepares the body for fight. They increase both the heart rate and the pressure at which the blood leaves the heart; they dilate bronchial passages and dilate coronary arteries; skin blood vessels constrict and there is an increase in metabolic rate. Also gastrointestinal system activity reduces, which leads to a sensation of 'butterflies in the stomach'.
- Lying close to the hypothalamus in the brain is an endocrine gland called the pituitary. In a stressful situation, the anterior hypothalamus activates the pituitary.
- The pituitary releases adrenocorticotrophic hormone (ACTH) into the blood, which then activates the outer part of the adrenal gland, the adrenal cortex.
- The adrenal cortex then synthesises cortisol, which increases arterial blood pressure, mobilises glucose and fats from the adipose (fat) tissues, reduces allergic reactions, reduces inflammation and can decrease lymphocytes (white blood cells) that are involved in dealing with invading particles or bacteria.
- Consequently, increased cortisol levels over a prolonged period of time lower the efficiency of the immune system. That's when we start to suffer from more colds and coughs than usual.
- The adrenal cortex releases aldosterone, which increases blood volume and subsequently blood pressure. Unfortunately, prolonged stress arousal over a period of time because of stress can lead to high blood pressure and a medical condition called essential hypertension.

- The pituitary also releases oxytocin and vasopressin, which contract smooth muscles such as the blood vessels.
- Oxytocin causes contraction of the uterus.
- Vasopressin increases the permeability of the vessels to water, therefore increasing blood pressure. It is important to maintain high blood pressure in a real fight or flight situation. It can lead to contraction of the intestinal musculature.
- The pituitary also releases a thyroid-stimulating hormone which stimulates the thyroid gland, which is located in the neck, to secrete thyroxin.
- Thyroxin increases the metabolic rate, raises blood sugar levels, increases the respiration, heart rate, blood pressure and intestinal motility. Increased intestinal motility can lead to diarrhoea. (Do note that an overactive thyroid gland under normal circumstances can be a major contributory factor in panic attacks. Too much thyroxin would normally require medication.)
- If the person perceives that the threatening situation has passed, then the PNS helps to restore the person to a state of equilibrium.

So you can see that the fight or flight stress response is real, and a number of complex physiological activities are occurring almost at once or in a sequence. Once the stressful event is over, we calm down with the help of the PNS. However, we evolved over many thousands of years to deal with real stressful scenarios where our life was on the line. Yet in modern society, often the stress response is triggered when our life is not threatened but when our ego is on the line, such as when we are giving a presentation or chairing a meeting.

# Activity 5
# Recall a stressful event

**Think back to the last time you became stressed about a specific event or situation. How quickly did you calm down?**

- **Immediately?**
- **In 5 minutes?**
- **In 10 minutes?**
- **In 30 minutes?**
- **In 1 hour?**
- **In 1 day?**
- **Still stressed now?**

We hope you are not still stressed by a recent event. However, many people do perceive every day of their life as stressful, and they keep the stress response or some parts of it active. The prolonged effect of the stress response is that the body's immune system is lowered and blood pressure is raised, which may lead to essential hypertension, headaches and more general infections such as colds. The adrenal gland may malfunction, which can result in tiredness, digestive difficulties with a craving for sweet, starchy food, sleep disturbances and dizziness.

## Summary

We have now covered what is stress.

- **Stress occurs when pressure exceeds our perceived ability to cope.**
- **Stress is real; it affects both the mind and body.**
- **Stress and pressure are different.**
- **Stress is not good for us.**

- We work at our optimum when under the right amount of pressure.
- Often the beliefs and attitudes we have developed over many years contribute or trigger stress at work, at home or in other situations.
- On a day-to-day basis, having an internal focus of control is good for our psychological health.
- Short-term stress is a natural response to dealing with threatening situations.
- Long-term stress can lead to a range of different physical and mental health conditions, and needs to be addressed and not ignored, as our case study illustrated.
- Often the stress response is triggered when our ego is put on the line.
- An internal locus of control is desirable.

At the end of each chapter we recommend that you make a note of the issues you wish to deal with and any useful stress-busting strategies that will help you to conquer or deal with stress. This will help you to develop your own stress-busting Stress Action Plan.

# A working model of stress, coping and resilience

This book will help you to understand and recognise stress in yourself and others, and then help you to choose stress-busting techniques and strategies to deal with stress. However, it is useful to be able to use a model of stress, coping and resilience to inform and underpin the choice of techniques.

We mentioned in the previous chapter that how we perceive a situation, and the expectations and attitudes we have to work or life in general, may trigger stress. The case study of the civil servant highlighted how his inflexible work ethic and high standards added so much pressure on him, and finally he could not take any more. Therefore our working model of stress needs to incorporate our real experience of life, and not just some academic treatise. This chapter will cover the model of stress, coping and resilience and symptoms of stress.

# A model of stress, coping and resilience

Let's consider a modern model of stress, which provides a useful framework that is broken down into a number of stages. We shall focus initially on the first three stages.

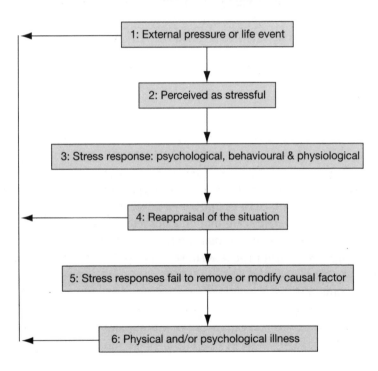

**Model of Stress**

1: External pressure or life event

2: Perceived as stressful

3: Stress response: psychological, behavioural & physiological

4: Reappraisal of the situation

5: Stress responses fail to remove or modify causal factor

6: Physical and/or psychological illness

© S Palmer, 2006

Source: adapted from Palmer and Strickland (1996).

**Figure 2.1**   A model of stress, coping and resilience

**Stage 1** is usually a life event or external pressure or demand that has come to the person's attention. It could be being asked to give a presentation to the board of directors, or needing to complete an important project within the deadline. Some of the more serious life events include being laid off work, bereavement, a serious accident or illness.

The amount of stress triggered by these events will vary from person to person, depending on how they are perceived by the individual. For example, a job promotion might be viewed by one person as an exciting challenge, whereas another person from the same office may see it as a poisoned chalice and then become anxious about it.

Complete the Life Events Questionnaire to help you analyse if you have suffered from too many life events recently.

# Activity 6
# Life Events Questionnaire

**Place a cross (X) in the 'Yes' column for each event which has taken place in the past two years. Then circle the number on the scale that best describes how upsetting the event crossed was to you, with 10 being the most upsetting and 1 the least upsetting.**

**Table 2.1**

| Event | Yes | Scale | | | | | | | | | |
|-------|-----|---|---|---|---|---|---|---|---|---|---|
| Bought house | | 1 | 2 | 3 | 4 | 5 | 6 | 7 | 8 | 9 | 10 |
| Sold house | | 1 | 2 | 3 | 4 | 5 | 6 | 7 | 8 | 9 | 10 |
| Moved house | | 1 | 2 | 3 | 4 | 5 | 6 | 7 | 8 | 9 | 10 |
| Major house renovation | | 1 | 2 | 3 | 4 | 5 | 6 | 7 | 8 | 9 | 10 |
| Separation from a loved one | | 1 | 2 | 3 | 4 | 5 | 6 | 7 | 8 | 9 | 10 |

| Event | Yes | Scale |
|---|---|---|
| End of relationship | | 1 2 3 4 5 6 7 8 9 10 |
| Got engaged | | 1 2 3 4 5 6 7 8 9 10 |
| Got married | | 1 2 3 4 5 6 7 8 9 10 |
| Marital problem | | 1 2 3 4 5 6 7 8 9 10 |
| Awaiting divorce | | 1 2 3 4 5 6 7 8 9 10 |
| Divorce | | 1 2 3 4 5 6 7 8 9 10 |
| Child started school/ nursery | | 1 2 3 4 5 6 7 8 9 10 |
| Increased nursing responsibility for elderly or sick person | | 1 2 3 4 5 6 7 8 9 10 |
| Problems with relatives | | 1 2 3 4 5 6 7 8 9 10 |
| Problems with friends/ neighbours | | 1 2 3 4 5 6 7 8 9 10 |
| Pet-related problems | | 1 2 3 4 5 6 7 8 9 10 |
| Work-related problems | | 1 2 3 4 5 6 7 8 9 10 |
| Change in nature of work | | 1 2 3 4 5 6 7 8 9 10 |
| Threat of redundancy | | 1 2 3 4 5 6 7 8 9 10 |
| Changed job | | 1 2 3 4 5 6 7 8 9 10 |
| Made redundant | | 1 2 3 4 5 6 7 8 9 10 |
| Unemployed | | 1 2 3 4 5 6 7 8 9 10 |
| Retired | | 1 2 3 4 5 6 7 8 9 10 |
| Increased or new bank loan/mortgage | | 1 2 3 4 5 6 7 8 9 10 |
| Financial difficulty | | 1 2 3 4 5 6 7 8 9 10 |
| Insurance problem | | 1 2 3 4 5 6 7 8 9 10 |

| Event | Yes | Scale |
|---|---|---|
| Legal problem | | I 2 3 4 5 6 7 8 9 10 |
| Emotional or physical illness of close family or relative | | I 2 3 4 5 6 7 8 9 10 |
| Serious illness of close family or relative requiring hospitalisation | | I 2 3 4 5 6 7 8 9 10 |
| Surgical operation experienced by family member or relative | | I 2 3 4 5 6 7 8 9 10 |
| Death of partner/ husband/ wife | | I 2 3 4 5 6 7 8 9 10 |
| Death of family member or relative | | I 2 3 4 5 6 7 8 9 10 |
| Death of close friend | | I 2 3 4 5 6 7 8 9 10 |
| Emotional or physical illness yourself | | I 2 3 4 5 6 7 8 9 10 |
| Serious illness requiring your own hospitalisation | | I 2 3 4 5 6 7 8 9 10 |
| Surgical operation on yourself | | I 2 3 4 5 6 7 8 9 10 |
| Pregnancy | | I 2 3 4 5 6 7 8 9 10 |
| Birth of baby | | I 2 3 4 5 6 7 8 9 10 |
| Birth of grandchild | | I 2 3 4 5 6 7 8 9 10 |
| Family member left home | | I 2 3 4 5 6 7 8 9 10 |
| Difficult relationship with children | | I 2 3 4 5 6 7 8 9 10 |
| Difficult relationship with parents | | I 2 3 4 5 6 7 8 9 10 |

Plot your total score on the scale below:

Low stress                    High stress
    1              50              100

During **Stage 2**, if the person perceives this event or pressure as stressful, then this triggers the 'fight or flight' stress response described in Chapter 1. The person might judge the situation negatively, by saying to him- or herself something like:

- **'Oh no! It's too difficult.'**
- **'It's awful. I couldn't stand it.'**
- **'I'm going to screw it up!'**
- **'I'm going to look so bad.'**
- **'I'm going to fail.'**
- **'I'm going to arrive late.'**

Sometimes people appraise a current situation by seeing negative images in their mind's eye:

- **An image of things going wrong, such as being unable to speak at a presentation, or being unable to answer difficult questions.**
- **Seeing work colleagues, family or friends laughing at them.**
- **Picturing a previous occasion when a task went wrong.**
- **Losing vital papers.**
- **Picturing the examination room.**
- **Seeing everybody looking at them when they arrive late for a meeting.**

However, if people believe they have the ability to deal with the demand, they perceive the situation as a challenge, and not as anything stressful. In fact, they may quite enjoy facing it, and feel excited. They may also believe that they have the coping skills, strategies and knowledge to be able to tackle any problems as they arise.

At **Stage 3**, the three key responses to stress are activated: the psychological, behavioural and physiological. The physiological response includes the release of stress hormones such as adrenaline and noradrenaline, which prepare the heart, lungs and major muscle groups for action – for either fight or flight. Fats and sugars are also released into the blood to provide energy.

However, in many situations in modern life there is no need to either fight or flee! Instead you may choose to think, feel and act in a manner which helps you to focus on the task or difficult situation that has arisen. For example, instead of procrastinating when given an important task by a senior manager at work, you could decide to focus on the task immediately, develop a priority list and get it completed within the deadline. This coping style helps you to be resilient.

Have another look now at the model of stress diagram, then do Activity 7 before reading on.

# Activity 7
# Self-assessment of your stress response

**Think back to the last time you became moderately stressed. (You can choose a very stressful event if you wish, as long as you do not overly upset yourself.) Tick the symptoms below that you recognise. If you are feeling stressed right now, tick those symptoms that you are currently experiencing.**

## Psychological

- angry;
- anxious, apprehensive, frightened, worrying thoughts;

- ashamed, embarrassed;
- depressed or feeling low;
- guilty;
- jealous;
- mood swings;
- reduced self-esteem, self-worth;
- feeling out of control, helpless;
- suicidal ideas;
- paranoid thinking;
- unable to concentrate;
- intrusive images or thoughts;
- negative images or pictures of situations going wrong;
- images of being out of control;
- images of suicide or death;
- increased daydreaming;
- having a poor self-image;
- nightmares.

## Behavioural

- passive behaviour;
- aggressive behaviour;
- irritability, snappiness;
- procrastination;
- increased alcohol consumption;
- increased caffeine consumption (in tea or coffee);
- comfort eating;
- disturbed sleep patterns (such as waking up early);
- withdrawing or sulking;
- clenched fists;
- banging a surface (like a table) with fists;
- compulsive or impulsive behaviour;
- 'checking' rituals;
- poor time management;
- reduced work performance;
- increased absenteeism from work;

- eating/talking/walking fast;
- increased accident-proneness;
- change in interest of sex;
- nervous tics.

## Physiological/physical

- dry mouth;
- clammy hands;
- frequent colds or other infections;
- palpitations or thumping heartbeat;
- breathlessness;
- tightness or pain in the chest;
- feeling faint or fainting;
- migraines;
- vague aches or pains;
- tension headaches;
- backaches;
- indigestion;
- diarrhoea;
- irritable bowel syndrome;
- constipation;
- skin complaints or allergies;
- asthma;
- excessive sweating;
- change to the menstrual pattern;
- rapid weight change;
- thrush or cystitis.

This exercise will help you to become aware of your responses to stress.

Which symptoms occurred first? In future, use these symptoms as an early-warning sign that you are possibly suffering from stress, and may benefit from some action on your part. If you are experiencing more than five of the above symptoms on a regular basis, you may wish to receive further advice from your GP. Some of the more serious symptoms, such as chest pains or suicidal ideas, need more urgent attention.

The list is just a guide. Some of the symptoms you have ticked may reflect a physical problem that needs medical assistance.

Now you have increased understanding of your response to stress, we can return to the model of stress. In **Stage 4**, people reappraise the original situation and decide whether or not they have successfully resolved it. If it is resolved or being managed successfully, the stress response is usually switched off. However, if a person believes he or she is not coping with the stress scenario, then some of the unhelpful psychological, behavioural and physiological responses may persist.

**Stage 5** focuses on whether the person has modified, removed or otherwise dealt with the external cause(s) of stress over a period of time. If the life event or external stress factor has not been successfully dealt with, physical or psychological illness(es) may ensue (**Stage 6**). If this occurs it can exacerbate an already difficult situation and feed back into the top of the stress diagram. For example, if a person has not successfully resolved problems at work and has under-performed for six months, it is very likely that his or her employer will provide negative feedback, or may even resort to a disciplinary procedure. This can have in turn a devastating effect on a person's self-esteem, and, as he or she becomes clinically depressed, his or her work deteriorates even more, leading finally to a long period of absenteeism or even dismissal.

# Helpful versus unhelpful troublesome negative emotions

In our working model of stress the emotional responses are included under the psychological response. It is useful to be aware of the emotions you are feeling when under stress, as some emotions are more helpful than others when tackling difficult situations. For example, feeling very anxious about attending an important meeting may lead to you choosing to avoid it, letting your colleagues down and giving an excuse. Feeling simply concerned about attending the meeting probably means that you will still turn up. You may even enjoy it, but you wouldn't know this if you didn't go. Feeling depressed about not getting a job promotion may lead you to withdraw from colleagues and become resentful, and to reduced performance at work. This could directly impact upon your future job prospects. Instead of feeling depressed, if you feel sad you are more likely to accept the situation but may still be motivated to apply for new jobs.

In most stressful situations you will usually suffer from a negative emotion. To feel nothing would be unrealistic! You would have to tell yourself, 'It doesn't matter.' Below is a table of helpful and unhelpful negative emotions. An activity follows that links in with the emotions.

## Helpful and unhelpful troublesome negative emotions

**Table 2.2**

| Inference* related to personal domain | Type of belief | Emotion |
| --- | --- | --- |
| Threat or danger | Unhelpful | Anxiety |
| Threat or danger | Helpful | Concern |
| Loss (with implications for future); failure | Unhelpful | Depression |
| Loss (with implications for future); failure | Helpful | Sadness |
| Breaking of own moral code | Unhelpful | Guilt |

| | | |
|---|---|---|
| Breaking of own moral code | Helpful | Remorse |
| Breaking of personal rule (other or self); other threatens self; frustration | Unhelpful | Damning anger |
| Breaking of personal rule (other or self); other threatens self; frustration | Helpful | Non-damning anger (or annoyance) |
| Personal weakness revealed publicly | Unhelpful | Shame/ embarrassment |
| Personal weakness revealed publicly | Helpful | Regret |
| Other betrays self (self non-deserving) | Unhelpful | Hurt |
| Other betrays self (self non-deserving) | Helpful | Disappointment |
| Threat to desired exclusive relationship | Unhelpful | Morbid jealousy |
| Threat to desired exclusive relationship | Helpful | Non-morbid jealousy |

Source: Palmer and Dryden (1995).

---

* An inference is an interpretation that goes beyond observable reality, but which gives meaning to it. It may be accurate or inaccurate.

# Activity 8
# Negative emotions

**Note down in the space below any negative emotions you feel when stressed and identify whether they are helpful or unhelpful. In other words, do they help or hinder you in achieving your goal(s)?**

**Which negative or troublesome emotions would you like to work on?**

**How could you tackle them the next time they occur?**

**Note down the unhelpful and stress-inducing thoughts and images that are associated with them. (Chapters 3 and 4 will help you change them.)**

As we approach the end of this chapter you may have realised that our working model is in fact a working model of stress, coping, performance, resilience and well-being. It highlights why some people become stressed whereas others can cope, perform well, are resilient and in good health.

# IMPORTANT: choice of interventions

How a person responds to stress is possibly the key to help him or her tackle stress. Let's take an example. If you procrastinate when given an important task, then you may need to focus on behavioural interventions such as time-management techniques: for example, develop a priority list or delegate less important tasks to staff or colleagues (see Chapter 5). You may have inflexibly high expectations such as 'I must do a perfect job', which may trigger goal-blocking high anxiety. Techniques that help to modify these thoughts and attitudes could be implemented (see Chapter 3). If you feel physically tense, a simple but effective relaxation technique could be beneficial (see Chapter 6). You may also have negative images in your mind's eye of not being able to give feedback to your colleagues about some aspect of a task or project. Whenever you see this particular image, it triggers more anxiety and stress. By using coping imagery whereby you see yourself coping with the situation, you may start to feel more confident (see Chapter 4).

The following chapters will help you to develop your own individual Stress Management Action Plan. If you take a quick look at Chapter 8 now, you will see the type of plan you may draw up for yourself.

## Summary

- **Our negative perceptions and appraisal of a situation, and not necessarily the situation in itself, may trigger the stress response.**
- **A model of stress provides a useful framework to understand how stress is triggered and how it can be successfully managed.**
- **The stress response occurs in a number of stages or steps.**
- **We have three key responses to stress: psychological, behavioural and physiological/physical.**
- **Long-term stress can lead to a number of more serious medical conditions.**
- **Life events perceived as stressful can mount up over time.**
- **Negative emotions can be helpful or unhelpful when dealing with a situation or task.**
- **Inferences may be accurate or inaccurate.**
- **Our responses to stress provide a clue to which techniques and strategies we could use to deal with it.**

# Changing your thinking

Now make some notes for yourself on what you have learnt. In the previous chapters we answered the question, 'What is stress?' It may have surprised you to learn that your perceptions about events, or your thinking style and attitudes, can also contribute to your levels of stress. In this chapter we shall show you how to examine your stress-inducing thinking errors and apply problem-solving thinking skills to most situations. We shall provide you with a toolkit of psychological techniques and strategies.

## Changing your thinking: it isn't a modern concept!

The influence of our perceptions over how stressed we become is not a modern concept. As the first-century philosopher Epictetus noted:

> People are disturbed not by things, but by the views which they take of them.

Centuries later, Shakespeare proffered a similar sentiment:

> [T]here is nothing either good or bad, but thinking makes it so.
>
> *Hamlet* II.ii

So what was their solution to dealing with stressful situations? Marcus Aurelius, a second-century Roman emperor and stoic philosopher, suggested that our internal 'assessor' could be challenged:

> Refuse its assessment, and all is well... Everything is what your opinion makes it; and that opinion lies with yourself.Renounce it when you will, and at once you have rounded the foreland and all is calm: a tranquil sea, a tideless haven.
>
> *Meditations*

During the past hundred years Sigmund Freud's psychoanalytical theory has greatly influenced Western society. The popularised interpretation of Freud has led many of us to believe that others, especially our parents, are to blame for how we feel and the way we act. Yet, if we take seriously the suggestion by the ancient philosophers that all we need to do is change or modify our thinking, then we are put firmly back in the driving seat, which enables us to deal with the inevitable stress and pressures of daily life.

According to Aurelius, by mentally reappraising a situation we can feel calmer and less stressed. This approach has received a lot of attention over the past 50 years from psychologists, who have undertaken many research studies to confirm that this method works for a range of stress-related problems.

## As simple as ABC!

So what exactly is the sequence of events that leads to stress? Five decades ago, Dr Albert Ellis, an internationally renowned psychologist, put forward the following ABC model.

## The ABC model of stress

A  Activating event or situation.

B  Beliefs about the event.

C  Consequences:
emotional, such as anxiety or anger;
behavioural, such as aggression or avoidance;
physiological, such as palpitations, sweaty/clammy hands.

Notice that this is similar to the first three stages of our model of stress (see page 28). This ABC model allows any situation that you become stressed about to be analysed. Activity 9 will hopefully illustrate this procedure.

# Activity 9
# Your thoughts when stressed

**Think back to the last time you became stressed. Perhaps you were stuck in a traffic queue or had just been asked by a colleague to give a presentation to the president of the company. Perhaps your computer had just crashed.**

1.  **Bring the incident back to mind as clearly as you can. What ideas or thoughts were going through your mind at the time?**
2.  **If you felt angry, did you label either yourself or the other person as a 'total idiot'?**
3.  **If you were anxious or stressed, did you think that the situation was 'awful' or 'terrible'?**
4.  **If you really did not like the situation, did you perhaps demand that things 'should be better' or that 'My boss must not treat me this way'?**
5.  **Perhaps you avoided the situation. If this was the case, did you tell yourself that 'I really can't stand it any more'?**

If you had these thoughts, did they help you to become less stressed or exacerbate the situation? In fact, did you become more able to solve problems or less able? We suspect the latter.

What insights, if any, did you glean from Activity 9? Most people we have done this exercise with are surprised at how their thoughts tended to make the situation worse. Regardless of the Activating event or stressful situation, psychologists have found that we hold a number of Beliefs that are self-defeating, task-interfering and goal-blocking in nature.

We have developed a simple self-assessment questionnaire to help you discover which of your beliefs can create or exacerbate stressful situations.

# Activity 10
# Stress-inducing beliefs indicator (SIBI)

**Do you recognise any of the following? The questions include both work and general beliefs. Circle the strength of your belief, where S represents 'strongly', M represents 'moderately' and W represents 'weakly'. Include in Question 25 any additional beliefs you hold that cause you further stress.**

**Table 3.1**

| | | | | |
|---|---|---|---|---|
| I | S | M | W | Events should go smoothly |
| 2 | S | M | W | Work must be exciting and stimulating |
| 3 | S | M | W | If I lost my job, it would be awful |
| 4 | S | M | W | If I lost my job, I could not bear it |
| 5 | S | M | W | My job is one of the most important things to me |

| 6 | S | M | W | I must perform well at all important tasks |
| 7 | S | M | W | My work should be recognised by others |
| 8 | S | M | W | I am indispensable at work |
| 9 | S | M | W | I must enjoy myself whatever I am doing |
| 10 | S | M | W | I must not get bored |
| 11 | S | M | W | I should not encounter problems |
| 12 | S | M | W | I should have the solitude I deserve |
| 13 | S | M | W | I must escape from responsibilities and demands |
| 14 | S | M | W | I should be treated fairly |
| 15 | S | M | W | I should be treated as special |
| 16 | S | M | W | I should be in control of all significant situations |
| 17 | S | M | W | Others should respect me |
| 18 | S | M | W | I should get on well with my friends and family |
| 19 | S | M | W | My children should do well in life |
| 20 | S | M | W | It things went badly, it would be awful |
| 21 | S | M | W | If things went badly, I could not stand it |
| 22 | S | M | W | Things never work out well for me |
| 23 | S | M | W | If things go wrong, those responsible are stupid, useless, idiots or failures |
| 24 | S | M | W | If I fail at a task, that proves I'm a failure or useless |
| 25 | S | M | W | Additional beliefs (write them in): |

**In our experience, if a person holds on strongly to one of the beliefs listed in the SIBI, when an event occurs that does not live up to expectations, stress may result.**

Therefore, the more beliefs you hold strongly or even moderately, the more stress you are likely to encounter. Do note that 'shoulds', 'musts', 'have tos', 'got tos' and similar demanding ideas you may hold are interchangeable. So if instead of a 'should' you use a 'must', this will still rate on the questionnaire. If you scored more than 10 strongly, it is very likely that you make many situations into potential stress scenarios! If more than 15, this section of the book is really for you. Even if you hold any of the above beliefs only moderately, under extremes of pressure you are likely to become quite stressed.

## Thinking errors

So what is the answer? Psychologists have identified 15 thinking errors that frequently contribute to stress and hinder successful problem solving. Our approach to dealing with them is in two stages:

1. Identify the thinking errors you most commonly use.
2. Use thinking skills to help modify the errors.

Activity 11 will help you undertake Stage 1 of our approach.

## Activity 11
## Thinking errors

Think back to the last time you were moderately stressed. Tick or highlight the following thinking errors that you recognise.

### All-or-nothing thinking

We view things in absolute, extreme terms without any shades of grey. Examples:

If a job is worth doing, it is worth doing really well.

My partner always makes the same mistakes.

# Labelling

**We 'globally rate' ourselves, others or the universe, as opposed to rating skills deficits or specific behaviours. Examples:**

Because I've failed my professional exams, this proves I am a total failure.

She's late again. That proves that she's incompetent.

# Focusing on the negative

**Instead of keeping life or events in perspective, we focus only on the negative aspects. Examples:**

Projects are always going wrong in my job.

Our parents are always causing us problems.

# Discounting the positive

**We choose to reframe anything positive as unimportant. Examples:**

When my manager gives me positive feedback she is only saying it to be nice. She doesn't really mean it.

My boyfriend only tells me that he loves me because he feels sorry for me. He doesn't really care.

# Mind-reading

**We infer from people's behaviour that they are either thinking or reacting negatively towards us. Examples:**

I'm sure my colleagues think that I can't undertake this project successfully.

My neighbour has ignored me again. He must have seen me in the garden. What have I done to upset him?

# Fortune-telling

**We predict the worst-case scenario, often by using insufficient evidence. Examples:**

We won't reach the deadline. I can see it all going wrong.

What's the point in going on holiday? The weather is bound to be awful and we'll get stuck in traffic again.

# Magnification or 'awfulising'

**We have a tendency to blow the significance of events out of proportion and make mountains out of molehills. Examples:**

If we don't reach that deadline, the outcome will be awful.

If she leaves me, it will be the end of my world.

# Minimisation

**We condemn ourselves for our shortcomings and make excuses for our successes or strengths. Examples:**

Getting the contract was nothing really. I'm not a good salesperson.

The exams I passed were easy ones. I was lucky.

# Emotional reasoning

**We evaluate situations by how we feel. Examples:**

I feel so angry, it proves that he treated me badly.

I feel so anxious about flying, it must be dangerous to fly.

# Blame

**Instead of taking any personal responsibility, we blame others for problems that have occurred. Examples:**

It's all the managing director's fault: she shouldn't have given me so much work.

Where are my keys? Who has moved them?

# Overgeneralisation

**We predict repeated outcomes on the basis of only one event. Examples:**

I've got off to a bad start today. That means the rest of the day will be a write-off too!

There is no point in applying for promotion as they have already turned me down once before.

# 'Personalisation'

**We blame ourselves unfairly for something for which we are not totally responsible. Examples:**

The team did not reach the target. It's all my fault.

My children have done badly at school and I am totally to blame.

## 'Demanding-ness'

This occurs when we hold unrealistic expectations or rigid and absolutist beliefs, which are usually expressed as 'shoulds', 'musts', 'got tos', 'have tos' and 'oughts'. Examples:

I must perform well regardless of the lack of resources.

My partner and I should never row with each other.

## 'Phoney-ism'

We fear others may find out that we are not the person we portray. Examples:

Even though so far I have given good lectures, one day I'll make a mistake and they will discover how incompetent I really am.

When my children grow up they will realise what a hopeless parent I was.

## 'I-can't-stand-it-itis'

We lower our tolerance for dealing with adversity or frustrating situations by telling ourselves that 'I can't stand it' or 'I can't bear it'. Examples:

I can't bear travelling on the Underground in the rush hour.

I can't stand small rooms or noisy children.

Activity 11 should have helped you recognise a number of thinking errors that you make. On reflection, do you think there are any that you regularly apply to many situations? In the next section we shall provide a range of thinking skills and strategies to help you challenge and modify these errors.

## The ABCDE of thinking errors and skills

Thinking skills can be used to help you challenge inaccurate perceptions about events or the 15 common thinking errors previously covered. But how do they fit into the ABC model of stress we described earlier? In fact, Dr Albert Ellis added two additional stages to his ABC model, which we highlight below:

The ABCDE model of stress

A   Activating event or situation.
B   Beliefs about the event.
C   Consequences:
    emotional, such as anxiety or anger;
    behavioural, such as aggression or avoidance;
    physiological, such as palpitations, sweaty/clammy hands.
D   Disputation of the beliefs at 'B'.
E   Effective new approach to deal with the activating event or problem at 'A'.

Once we note down our stress-inducing thoughts (SITs) and thinking errors at 'B', we can start to dispute or challenge them at 'D' and subsequently develop new stress-coping statements along with an effective new approach to help us deal with the problem.

# Activity 12
# Thinking errors audit

So far, so good! The hard work starts now. To help you practise the thinking skills, we suggest that you think about either a previous stress scenario or a current problem you are stressed about. Note down your stress-inducing and task-interfering beliefs. Complete the table below by noting down the thinking errors you recognise. For example, 'I always make mistakes' would be written in the 'All-or-nothing' box. 'I'm useless' would go under 'labelling'. (You may wish to include thinking errors that you regularly make too.)

**Table 3.2**

| Thinking errors | Your example |
| --- | --- |
| All-or-nothing thinking | |
| Labelling | |
| Focusing on the negative | |
| Discounting the positive | |
| Mind-reading | |
| Fortune-telling | |
| Magnification or 'awfulising' | |
| Minimisation | |
| Emotional reasoning | |
| Blame | |
| Overgeneralisation | |
| 'Personalisation' | |
| 'Demanding-ness' | |
| Phoney-ism | |
| 'I-can't-stand-it-itis' | |

Now you have completed Activity 12, you should be in a position to start tackling your thinking errors or incorrect perceptions. Below we list a few methods to help you modify your stress-inducing thinking. Use one or more of these thinking skills to help challenge your thinking errors.

## Relative thinking

If you are perceiving events in extreme terms, such as 'excellent versus poor', try to introduce shades of grey. Find some middle ground to help you keep the situation in perspective.

For example, instead of thinking 'She never reaches her targets', be more realistic: 'Although this year she has failed to reach two targets on time, she has successfully achieved eight others.' Instead of thinking, 'If a job's worth doing, it's worth doing very well', introduce a less extreme attitude: 'Within the time and resources I have available, I'll do an acceptable job.'

## Befriend yourself

If a member of your family or a colleague makes an error, how do you react? Most people are supportive; therefore we can say they possess befriending skills. However, how often do you use these skills on yourself? When you make a mistake can you accept yourself, or do you become ultra-critical and metaphorically beat yourself up?

For example, instead of thinking 'That was a hopeless presentation. That proves I'm totally useless', step back from the situation and describe it more accurately: 'Some aspects of my presentation were not particularly good. However, this does not prove that I'm totally useless. In fact, I now know what areas I can focus on to improve my next presentation.'

## De-labelling

When you describe either yourself or somebody else as 'a total failure', 'useless', 'stupid', 'an idiot', 'a fool' or a similar 'global rating', examine your idea more closely. Is it really an accurate description? To be a 'total failure', what would a person have to do all the time, day and night? Think carefully before you answer. Yes, you may have the correct answer! The person would have to fail at *absolutely everything* to be a 'total failure'. Obviously this is extremely difficult, if not impossible, to achieve.

For example, instead of thinking, 'I have failed my exam, therefore I am a complete failure', focus on the behavioural deficit, and avoid going as far as a global rating of yourself: 'All it proves is that I've failed my exam – no more, no less. Tough; too bad; I can survive this hassle.' Another example is to think, 'Although I've acted stupidly, this does not mean I'm stupid.'

When you are angry about another person's action, again rate the *behaviour* and not the person: 'Although my manager has interpersonal skills deficits, it does not make him a total idiot.'

## Broaden the picture

Instead of focusing on the negative and discounting the positive, start concentrating on more realistic and positive aspects of a situation. When things go wrong, individuals too often blame either themselves (personalisation) or an innocent bystander. So, whatever situation you find yourself in, attempt to broaden the picture when blame enters the equation. First, write down all the different factors or people involved. Second, draw a circle on a large sheet of paper. Third, using the circle, draw a pie diagram, with each section approximately equating to the fault or responsibility of the different factors or people involved. Finally, whatever is left of the pie diagram is probably your responsibility.

This technique is often used when an employee totally blames him- or herself for not reaching a work deadline or target, or when parents blame themselves for their teenager underperforming in school exams. Let's look at a completed example.

## Case study: 'It's all my fault'

Situation: Jayne worked with five colleagues in a small department. They had failed to meet an important deadline on a particular project. She totally blamed herself, and started to feel down and unmotivated. Her key thinking errors were emotional reasoning and personalisation. Figure 3.1 illustrates her perceived '100 per cent' responsibility.

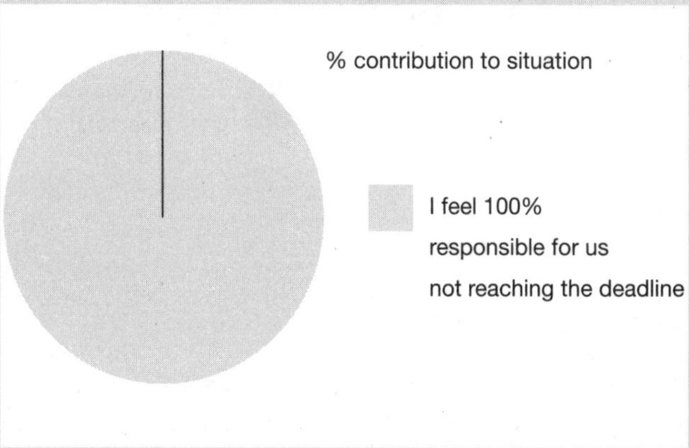

% contribution to situation

I feel 100% responsible for us not reaching the deadline

**Figure 3.1**

Jayne's coach suggested that she could 'broaden the picture' by noting down in a pie chart all the relevant details. She soon realised she was not completely responsible (see Figure 3.2) and there were in fact other factors that had contributed to them not meeting the deadline.

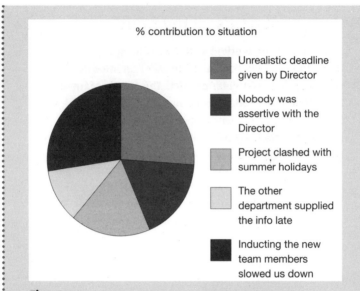

% contribution to situation

- Unrealistic deadline given by Director
- Nobody was assertive with the Director
- Project clashed with summer holidays
- The other department supplied the info late
- Inducting the new team members slowed us down

**Figure 3.2**

## The blame game

Broadening the picture can also be used if you blame everybody else for your problems. The first pie diagram would state that everybody or everything else was 100 per cent responsible. Then in the second pie diagram you can insert how responsible you are. A typical blame game problem we hear in coaching is 'My manager gives me too much work.' We have even found that over 50 per cent of our clients have not told their managers or supervisors that they have been given too much work.

The general questions we ask to help our coaching clients gain insight are:

- What responsibility do you have regarding this particular problem?

- What are all the factors that are involved with this particular problem?
- Can your manager read minds? Whose responsibility is it to tell your manager that you have been given too much work?

You may need to think of additional questions you can ask yourself that are relevant to the issue involved. Seldom is only one person repsonsible in any situation. Even with workplace accidents, so often it was the system, or lack of system, that allowed an accident to occur, and this often involves joint responsibility.

## Activity 13
## Who is reponsible?

1. Think back to the last time you totally blamed either yourself or another person for a particular problem or outcome. You may wish to use a current issue.
2. Note down below all the factors that relate to the issue concerned:

   a)

   b)

   c)

   d)

   e)

   f)

3.   Complete the empty pie diagram (Figure 3.3), allocating the approximate percentage of responsibility either you or others have or had in the situation:

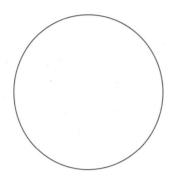

**Figure 3.3**

4.   Now you have completed this exercise, was it only you to blame or one other person or organisation? Hopefully this technique will help you to see problems from a larger perspective instead of either beating yourself up or wasting time and emotional energy just blaming others.

A postscript to this activity. Managers or supervisors who have been trained to work as coaches at work may find this technique particularly useful with staff or teams who are more focused on the blame game than on just focusing on the task concerned. In our experience some organisations, departments or teams have a blame culture that seriously needs addressing, and this technique can be used as an organisation moves towards a coaching culture.

## Seek evidence

Avoid mind-reading or making assumptions. Look for the evidence for and against your stress-inducing ideas. This may involve asking your family, friends or colleagues for feedback about something you may have done, such as giving a presentation, completing a task, or some personal issue. If you believe that your manager or partner really does not like what you are doing or have done, ask him or her to share his or her thoughts with you. Avoid 'beating about the bush'. Ask a direct question. You can also challenge your thinking behaviourally.

For example, if you believe that 'I can't stand queuing', when you next find yourself in a situation when you have to queue, join the longest one. Instead of making yourself angry and wound up, remind yourself that 'Although I don't like queuing, I'm living proof that I can stand it!'

## Think more flexibly

Dogmatic, inflexible, absolutist and demanding beliefs trigger high levels of stress. Introduce flexible beliefs such as preferences, desires and wants into your repertoire.

For example, instead of thinking 'I must perform well', 'I should achieve my deadlines regardless of the lack of resources', or 'My children have to do well at school', attempt to become more flexible in your thinking style. 'It's strongly preferable to perform well, but realistically I don't have to.' 'Although it's highly desirable to achieve my deadlines, with the current lack of resources I can only do my best.' Or, 'Of course I want my children to do well, but demanding that they have to can only make the situation worse. Let's give myself and them a break.'

## Demagnify or 'deawfulise'

Whatever the situation, if you blow it out of proportion, you are very likely to increase your stress levels. Of course events may be difficult to deal with, or even be plain bad, but are they really 'the end of the world', 'horrendous', 'awful', 'horrible'? Seldom are events we face on a day-to-day basis that bad. To examine stress scenarios dispassionately, we recommend that you distance yourself from your immediate stress-inducing thinking to help you 'see the wood from the trees'.

For example, 'It's really terrible that I failed my driving test.' Now, if you examine the situation just described, all that has happened is that a person has failed a driving test. This may be a hassle, but keeping it in perspective, is it really a terrible event? No! However, in their own mind the person has elevated a hassle into a horror, which leads to unnecessary stress. A realistic view would be, 'I've failed my driving test. Tough; too bad. It's just a great inconvenience – no more, no less.'

## Keep emotions in their place

As we described earlier, when people make the emotional reasoning thinking error, they evaluate a situation on the strength of their feelings and not on the situation itself. In the previous section on emotional reasoning (page 49), we described two classic examples where emotions can cloud a person's judgement. We suggest that it is important to remind yourself that just because you are feeling a strong emotion such as anxiety, it does not necessarily mean that you are in a threatening situation nor have been treated badly when you are feeling angry.

For example, tell yourself, 'Just because I'm feeling anxious it does not mean that flying is dangerous,' or 'Perhaps I feel very angry because I misinterpreted my partner's actions. I'll ask him what it was all about.'

To summarise, thinking skills are used to promote realistic rather than positive thinking. Things may be bad, but seldom are they really awful, unless we allow our thinking to make them so!

# Helpful challenging questions

Now that we have introduced you to some of the key thinking errors and thinking skills, you may wonder what we do as psychologists when we are either coaching or counselling individuals who are feeling stressed. In addition to the skills we have discussed in the previous section, we also help such people to become their own self-coaches. Once they have identified the ABCs of the problem according to Dr Albert Ellis's model, we provide them with a list of helpful questions they can use to challenge their own stress-inducing ideas. You can give this self-help approach a go now, in Activity 14. Here we also introduce the final part of the model: 'F' for Focus.

# Activity 14
# Helpful challenging questions

This activity involves a number of steps:

Step 1   Think of a situation you are or have been stressed about (for example, missing a deadline). Note this down in the first column on the worksheet provided (Table 3.3). This is your Activating event.

Step 2   Next, note down on the worksheet in the third column both how you felt and your behaviour – for example 'anxious' or 'procrastinating'. These are your Consequences.

Step 3   Now imagine the situation at A and get into the feelings you described at C. When you are feeling stressed, note down your stress-inducing thoughts (SITs) that are associated with how you feel. These are your Beliefs. Some of these may be unhelpful and self-defeating, because they hinder you and do not help you attain your goals.

**Table 3.3**

| Activating event or situation | Stress-inducing thoughts (SITs) or beliefs | Consequences | Stress-alleviating thoughts (SATs) (disputing the beliefs at B) | Effective new approach to deal with the activating event | Focus |
|---|---|---|---|---|---|
| A | B | C | D | E | F |
| | | | | | |
| | | | | | |
| | | | | | |
| | | | | | |

Step 4   Let us now move on to Disputation. This is when you dispute, examine or challenge the SITs or beliefs you noted down in Step 3 here, your B. Watch out for your thinking errors. To help you challenge your beliefs, we have provided below (pages 63–64) the list of 'helpful challenging questions' we use with our stressed clients.

## Helpful challenging questions

- Is it logical?
- Would a scientist agree with my logic?
- Where is the evidence for my belief?
- Where is the belief written (apart from inside my own head!)?
- Is my belief realistic?
- Would my friends and colleagues agree with my idea?
- Does everybody share my attitude? If not, why not?
- Am I expecting myself or others to be perfect, as opposed to fallible, human beings?
- What makes the situation so awful, terrible or horrible?
- Am I making a mountain out of a molehill?
- Will it seem this bad in 1, 3, 6 or 12 months' time?
- Will it be important in 2 years' time?
- Is it really as bad a problem as a serious accident or a close bereavement?
- Am I exaggerating the importance of this problem?
- Am I fortune-telling again, with little evidence that the worst-case scenario will actually happen?
- If I 'can't stand it' or 'can't bear it', what will really happen?
- If I can't stand it, will I really fall apart?
- Am I concentrating on my (or others') weaknesses and neglecting my (or others') strengths?

- Am I agonising about how things should be instead of dealing with them as they are?
- Where is this thought or attitude getting me?
- Is my belief helping me to attain my goal(s)?
- Is my belief goal-focused and problem-solving?
- If a friend made a similar mistake, would I be so critical?
- Am I thinking in all-or-nothing terms? Is there any middle ground?
- Am I labelling myself, somebody or something else? Is this logical, and a fair thing to do?
- Just because a problem has occurred, does it mean that I am (it is, they are) stupid, a failure, useless or hopeless?
- Am I placing demands (such as 'shoulds' or 'musts') on myself or others? If I am, is this proving helpful and constructive?
- Am I taking things too personally?
- Am I blaming others unfairly just to make myself (temporarily) feel better?

Select the questions that may help you to challenge your beliefs at B (in the ABC model of stress). It is important to ask yourself the question and then ponder on the possible answer for a while. It is also worth noting that the questions could easily be boiled down to three main types:

1. Is the belief logical (does it make logical sense)?
2. Is the belief realistic (empirically correct)?
3. Is the belief helpful (for instance, assisting you to reduce stress, improve performance and achieve your goals)?

Once you have asked yourself the appropriate questions, modify the belief you held at B to one that is more logical, realistic and helpful. For example, attempt to shift your attitude from 'Missing the deadline is really awful' to 'Missing the deadline is a pain, but hardly awful. Frankly, I'm making a mountain out of a molehill' (a realistic and helpful stress-reducing belief). Note down this new belief in column D.

Step 5    You have almost finished. Now note down your Effective new approach to dealing with the situation. For example, make up for lost time by finishing the task now and don't waste any more time fretting, moaning with colleagues, surfing the internet or comfort eating!

Step 6    Have you learnt anything from this whole process? On the worksheet, F is for Focus. There are two aspects of focus. One is staying focused on the existing task or problem, but there is also the Future Focus. In other words, what you have learnt from the ABCDE process that you can remember the next time a similar problem occurs.

Reflect on this for your example and then complete the last column on your worksheet.

NB    You can use Table 3.4 if your particular problem relates more to performance than stress.

## Case study: Ron, the procrastinating perfectionist!

Ron encountered difficulty giving presentations at work and also on his college course. In the case example illustrated in the completed worksheet (Table 3.5), Ron focused on his forthcoming work presentation. When completing these worksheets it is usually beneficial just to focus on one particular issue or problem at a time.

**Table 3.4**

| Target problem | Performance interfering thoughts (PITs) | Emotional/ behavioural reaction | Performance enhancing thoughts (PETs) | Effective and new approach to problem | Focus |
|---|---|---|---|---|---|
| A | B | C | D | E | F |
| | | | | | |
| | | | | | |
| | | | | | |
| | | | | | |

Let's examine Ron more closely. He was a rigid perfectionist who would regularly 'should' or 'must' himself with strong, demanding imperatives. For example, he would tell himself, 'I must give a good presentation'. He would use mind-reading and label himself as 'totally useless'. He also awfulised and saw the outcome as terrible. This style of thinking is almost guaranteed to create performance stress if a person considers that the situation is important. The good news is that this type of performance stress largely emanates from within, and therefore a person can learn to deal with it quite rapidly using the techniques described in this book.

Notice how he finally decided that the lesson for the future was to realise that he could become a lot better at presentations if he stopped avoiding doing them. However, the paradox for perfectionists who become very anxious and stressed about giving presentations is that they seldom grasp opportunities to give them. Whenever possible they would rather avoid them! Yet, if they had more practice, then it is very likely their performance stress would decrease and their presentation skills would improve.

One last point: to improve confidence we need skills practice. However, coping imagery can also increase confidence or self-efficacy, in that we develop strategies to deal with potential problems before they arise. This helps our belief in ourselves that 'we can do it'. Coping imagery is covered in Chapter 4. If you are really keen to learn about it go to page 92 now.

**Table 3.5** Ron's completed worksheet

| Activating event or situation | Stress-inducing thoughts (SITs) or beliefs | Consequences | Stress-alleviating thoughts (SATs) (disputing the beliefs at B) | Effective new approach to deal with the activating event | Focus |
|---|---|---|---|---|---|
| A | B | C | D | E | F |
| Giving a presentation at work | I'm going to screw up (fortune-telling) | Anxious and stressed | How do I know if I'm going to screw up? I'm not clairvoyant! | Need to focus now on preparation of the presentation. This will give me a better chance of success. | The lesson for the future is to realise that I could become a lot better at presentations if I stop avoiding them. |
| | I must give a good presentation (demands upon self) | Anxious and worried; procrastinates | It's strongly preferable to give a good presentation but I don't have to | Stop procrastinating. Make a priority list of what I need to do. Do, don't stew! | |

**Table 3.5** continued

| Activating event or situation | Stress-inducing thoughts (SITs) or beliefs | Consequences | Stress-alleviating thoughts (SATs) (disputing the beliefs at B) | Effective new approach to deal with the activating event | Focus |
|---|---|---|---|---|---|
| A | B | C | D | E | F |
| | It will be terrible if I screw up (awfulising) | Anxious and stressed | In reality I doubt that the world will stop. I'm unlikely to lose my job. | Stay focused on the task | In future start to use coping imagery to help me deal with potential problems. |
| | They will think I'm totally useless (labelling and mind-reading) | A bit low | I've spent years avoiding giving presentations, so I need more practice. However, if I do screw up it doesn't mean I'm totally useless. It just means that I lack presentation skills – not a big deal. | I'll use evaluation forms so I can really find out what they think. | |

# 'Pros and cons'

Another good method to help deal with the psychological slings and arrows that we hurl at ourselves when we are under pressure or stress is a 'pros and cons' analysis of our stress-inducing thoughts (SITs). Writing up a 'pros and cons' list is a fairly straightforward procedure, often used in the work environment to help managers decide what particular approach to take when attempting to solve a range of difficulties. We have modified it to focus on the validity and usefulness of the ideas or beliefs people hold when stressed.

The completed form highlights Jayne's problem. She is a perfectionist who wishes to start revising for her forthcoming professional exams. As is often the case with rigid perfectionists, she is procrastinating and not getting down to her studying. This situation is, furthermore, repeated at work when she has important deadlines to meet. Again, many perfectionists claim that they work best at the eleventh hour or under pressure. Perhaps you do too! But we would argue that such people are not then at their best and, what's more, are very likely to make errors late at night. We can think of cases when rigid perfectionists have been so tired and flustered at midnight or minutes before a meeting that they forgot to spell-check important reports or documents. Their perfectionistic approach ends up looking unprofessional. Let's look closely at Jayne's 'pros and cons' analysis, laid out in the worksheet (Table 3.6).

Perhaps you recognise in yourself all or at least some of Jayne's belief, 'I must not fail my exams. If I did, I would be a failure and that would be awful.'

## Table 3.6

| Problem: | Procrastinating, not studying |
| --- | --- |
| **Belief:** | I must not fail my exams. If I did, I would be a failure, and that would be awful. |
| **Goal:** | To start studying this morning. |

| Advantages | Disadvantages |
| --- | --- |
| I shall do my best. | I am spending all my time worrying about failing my exams. |
| I produced a really good plan for how I'm going to start on my revision. | I've spent hours and hours planning my revision but I still have not started it properly yet! |
| My belief helps me to motivate me. | It also helps to make me feel so anxious that I can't concentrate on my studies. I spent my time worrying about becoming a failure and how awful that would be. In addition, I've spent many years of my life avoiding doing things that I might fail in. |
| My family will be so proud of me if I get a good pass. | If I stay anxious and stressed, I won't do well and they won't be proud of me. |
| My study is now spotless and the files on my PC are all in order. | The only way I can calm down is to tidy things up. But this is just wasting my precious time, which I can't afford to lose. I've even cleaned the kitchen floor twice today! |

© Centre for Coaching (2009)

## Activity 15
## Completing a 'pros and cons' form

To undertake this exercise we recommend that you complete the blank pros and cons form (Table 3.7) or use an A4 sheet instead. Start with noting the nature of your problem or issue, then include your most stress-inducing belief, and finally write your goal underneath. Then complete it in the same manner as Jayne, noting down your pros first and then the corresponding cons.

Once you have included all the 'pros and cons' you may wish to ask a friend or colleague to help you brainstorm additional ones. Once you have finished making the list, decide whether it is worth modifying your idea to a belief that is more flexible, self-helping and task-oriented. In Jayne's case she developed a new belief:

Although it's strongly preferable not to fail my exam, if I do then it doesn't prove I'm a failure, because I have many other worthwhile attributes. It may be a hassle, but it certainly isn't awful or the end of the world. I might as well just start revising now.

This is a simple yet useful exercise that can be used with colleagues, partners and indeed children that needs only time, paper and a pen!

## Table 3.7

| Problem: |
|---|
| Belief: |
| Goal: |

| Advantages | Disadvantages |
|---|---|
| | |

# Stress thought record

For some stress-triggering situations there is no need to use the six-column ABCDEF form we have discussed. With practice, you may be able to 'cut to the chase' by using a two-column stress thought record instead. This involves making a note of what stress-inducing thoughts (SITs) or thinking errors you are experiencing for a particular issue or problem. Once you have identified which SITs are exacerbating your stress, you can begin to apply the thinking skills discussed previously, and develop stress-alleviating thoughts (SATs) to counter them. (The SITs and SATs method was developed by Neenan and Palmer, Centre for Stress Management.) A completed example is shown.

**Table 3.8**

| **Problem:** Possible redundancy | **Goal:** to reduce my stress levels and deal with financial concerns. |
|---|---|
| **Stress-inducing thoughts (SITs)** | **Stress-alleviating thoughts (SATs)** |
| Redundancy could impact upon my family and finances | Worrying won't decrease the likely redundancy – it will probably make it worse if anything. |
| | I have lots of skills – if I was made redundant I shouldn't have too much of a problem finding other employment. |
| This shouldn't happen to me. | Why shouldn't it? The reality is that cutbacks may have to be made. |
| The company should look after its staff. | The company has everyone to consider – it's not personal to me. |

| | |
|---|---|
| They are treating me so badly after all the years I've worked for them. | Are they? I'm taking this rather personally. It won't help me!<br><br>**Other ideas**<br><br>When worry occurs at work, tell myself that, 'there's nothing I can do about it right now'.<br><br>Perhaps use 10 minutes' worry time in the evening before dinner.<br><br>Use problem-solving skills to work on the employment situation and revise the financial situation. Ask for break in mortgage payments.<br><br>Update CV and scan papers for jobs. |

© Centre for Stress Management (2006).

# Activity 16
# Completing a stress thought record to combat stress

1. Think of the situation or event you are stressed about. Note down the problem on the blank stress thought record (STR) provided (Table 3.9).
2. Note down on the STR your goal or goals which relate to this problem.
3. Now think about the problem. When are you becoming stressed about it? What are you telling yourself? Note down these SITs in the first column.

4. Now think of more helpful alternatives (SATs) to the SITs. Note the SATs down opposite the corresponding SITs in the second column.

5. Once you have finished developing the SATs, note down any additional ideas or specific tasks or strategies to help you to achieve your desired goal(s).

**Table 3.9**

| Problem: | Goal: |
|---|---|
| Stress-inducing thoughts (SITS) | Stress-alleviating thoughts (SATs) |
|  |  |
|  |  |
|  |  |
|  |  |

# Dealing with your own anger

The stress flight emotional response is anxiety, whereas the stress fight emotional response is anger. Feeling angry in some situations may be adaptive and helpful, such as in a real fighting situation, although on many occasions it would be preferable to remain relatively calm, especially in the workplace or with your family.

However, when you are under too much pressure at work or at home, it is all too easy to become excessively angry. This does not usually help relationships, your health, in particular blood pressure, or your remaining focused on tasks or projects. If you believe that it is having an unhelpful impact on these areas, your anger may be worth tackling.

# Activity 17
# Feeling an emotion, any emotion

**This is a quick activity which is worth doing to illustrate an important point.**

**Without any thought or image or picture in your head, attempt now to feel an emotion such as anger, guilt or anxiety. Spend 30 seconds doing this exercise.**

**How did you get on?**

For most people it is almost impossible to feel an emotion unless they have a thought or image in their mind. This is an important observation, as it highlights how important our thoughts or mental images or visualisations are in contributing to stress and emotions. However, using imagery and thinking skills can also help to reduce or control anger.

There are behavioural skills that also help us to stay calmer in difficult situations, such as assertion skills. These are covered in Chapter 5.

We now consider anger-activating and anger-deactivating thoughts. Similar to the other cognitive techniques in this chapter, if we can identify our anger-activating thoughts, we can then counter them with anger-deactivating thoughts as the next case study will highlight.

## Case study: Angry John

John was becoming very angry with his colleagues, who he believed were not 'pulling their weight' on a particular project. With his coach Nick, he noted down his anger-activating thoughts on a worksheet (see below) and then with the help of his coach he developed alternative anger-deactivating thoughts. Once they had finished this, they then developed constructive ideas and included them in the worksheet.

**Table 3.10**

| Anger-activating thoughts | Anger-deactivating thoughts |
|---|---|
| Why don't they pull their weight? | Perhaps I'm over-generalising. |
| They don't care about the project. | Just because they are not always talking about the project does not mean they don't care. |
| We will get the project in late. | I'll go over the schedule again and check whether we are all keeping to our agreed deadlines. |
| I can't stand their inefficiency. | If they have been inefficient, I've stood it for the past two years! |

| | |
|---|---|
| They really should focus on this project. | At the meetings they seemed focused. |
| They are complete idiots. | It's not true. They wouldn't have their qualifications and their jobs if they were complete idiots. |
| | **Other constructive ideas:**<br><br>Perhaps I'm over-reacting.<br><br>Am I taking this project too seriously? |
| | I'll discuss my concerns in a calm manner at the next team meeting and get people's feedback. |

# Activity 18
# Deactivating your own anger

Think of a situation or person (or both!) that you feel angry about. Note down on the worksheet (Table 3.11) the anger-activating thoughts and/or images that you have, and then develop alternative anger-deactivating thoughts so you feel less angry and stressed and more task-focused instead. Include additional constructive ideas too, that may help you to deal with the problem.

## Useful tip

In the case study John had the assistance of his coach. If you encounter difficulty developing anger-deactivating thoughts or beliefs, then you may want to ask a colleague or friend you trust to help you. Obviously don't choose a colleague who also gets angry easily, as he or she may share similar anger-activating thoughts to you! Choose a person who seems not to become wound up about issues, as he or she might use more stress-alleviating or anger-deactivating thoughts.

Table 3.11

| Anger-activating thoughts | Anger-deactivating thoughts |
|---|---|
| | |
| | |
| | |
| | |
| | |
| | Other constructive ideas: |
| | |
| | |

# Overcoming the self-esteem trap

In Western society we have found that one of the main causes of stress for people of all ages is having a strong belief in the concept of self-esteem. This may sound somewhat remarkable, yet we see it daily in our work. In this section we focus on self-esteem and the healthier alternative known as self-acceptance.

## Activity 19
## Self-esteem

**Spend the next five minutes noting down on paper how you, your friends, colleagues and family build up their self-esteem. You may think that you are OK as a person for a number of reasons. State these reasons.**

Activity 19 was probably an easy exercise to undertake. We have found that the main 'external' factors that people in Western society use to enhance their self-esteem are these (Palmer, 1997):

- **achievement, such as passing exams;**
- **having a good relationship with significant others;**
- **having a rewarding and satisfactory job or career;**
- **owning property;**
- **possessing excellent physical characteristics;**
- **being competent in personally significant areas;**
- **being a good parent/grandparent/colleague/friend;**
- **being a good lover, partner and so on;**
- **being loved by a significant other;**
- **being approved of by significant others;**
- **practising a religious faith.**

Essentially, people tend to 'dis-esteem' themselves when they lose something personally significant, such as a job, a partner, good health or property, and conversely esteem themselves more highly when they have or acquire something personally significant, such as a good job, an attractive partner, a good physique or a high IQ. So when a person says, 'I'm OK because ...', that person is probably into the self-esteem trap. In concrete terms, some of the common examples of this trap are thinking that you are OK because:

- **I'm attractive.**
- **I have a great physique.**
- **I've got a good job.**
- **I never lose my temper.**
- **I'm a good parent.**
- **I'm good in bed.**
- **I've passed my exams.**
- **I'm well qualified.**
- **I have many friends.**
- **I have a good sense of humour.**
- **I am close to my family.**
- **I have a decent car.**

However, all living human beings get older and possibly less attractive (look in the mirror and notice the thinning hair or wrinkles!); some may lose their job or have to retire; others may have negative personal attributes, be at times deficient in their parenting skills, lose their property, fail exams or lose friends through arguments or death. This is just a small selection of relevant personal aspects. We are sure that you can think of many more.

Thus, the philosophy of esteeming one's self can set us up for potential problems in the future when adversity in almost any form strikes. It is no surprise that recent research has shown how teachers often blame poor media coverage and lack of governmental support as major contributory factors leading to reduced self-esteem and self-worth. So what is the alternative?

## From the trap to greater self-acceptance

With self-esteem you feel good about yourself when life is going well, but bad when life is not going well. To avoid these ups and downs and the rollercoaster ride of self-esteem, we suggest that learning greater self-acceptance can reduce much stress and literally provide people with a new sense of personal freedom. The concept of self-acceptance acknowledges that one of the key aspects that makes us human is that we are fallible and definitely not perfect. Therefore we could turn the earlier statement on its head by telling ourselves:

I'm OK just because I exist.

Although it may sound rather extreme, spend a few moments thinking about this idea. Would it take the stress out of many of those competitive situations that you have encountered or when you have lost something significant in your life? Another helpful self-accepting belief might be this:

I can accept myself, warts and all, with a strong preference to improve myself, even though realistically I don't have to.

This belief is even better. You could learn to accept yourself even with all your faults. However, we have found that it is important, especially for people with strong, rigid, perfectionist beliefs, still to keep a strong desire to perform well. Preferences, wants and desires are very healthy as long as people do not demand that they 'must' achieve their desires. This helps the concept of self-acceptance to remain realistic, unlike self-esteem.

Striving for excellence, which we are encouraged to do at work or in other settings, is not the same as demanding 100 per cent perfection, which is seldom attained. You will probably have observed in rigid perfectionists that they are rarely happy with what either they or others have done. The clue is in what they say once they or you have finished an important task:

> It was OK.
> I could have done better.
> You could have done better.
> It was satisfactory.

As managers or parents they often demotivate their staff or children without realising it.

Another helpful self-accepting belief may be:

> I am too complex to be rated.

This is a pretty remarkable idea that takes the stress out of many situations. Consider the implications when we translate this into a concrete example. Instead of 'Because I have failed my exam I am a total failure' (a global rating of self that leads to self-defeating stress, anxiety and depression), the alternative becomes, 'Because I have failed my exam, all it proves is that I have exam skills deficits' (the rating of skills, leading to healthy and realistic disappointment but still retaining motivation). The person could add, 'and I possibly could have spent more time revising'.

To conclude, the concept of self-acceptance is more robust than the self-esteem concept, as self-acceptance is realistic, logical and pragmatic. You can rate your skills or certain aspects of yourself, but globally rating yourself does not add up!

## Accepting others but not their behaviour

Think of the times when you have become angry about another person's behaviour, such as that of your partner, child, parent, colleague, manager or maybe even another driver. Did you globally rate and label them as:

- totally useless;
- lazy bastard;
- total jerk;
- a complete waste of space;
- stupid;
- complete idiot;  or 'xxxxxxx!'?

Or perhaps you kept relatively calm and accepted their fallibility by just rating such aspects as these:

- **On this occasion my child acted stupidly but this does not mean she is stupid.**
- **This is more evidence that he is fallible.**
- **My father has interpersonal skills deficits.**
- **The driver is exhibiting driving skills deficits.**
- **She may have acted idiotically but that does not make her an idiot.**
- **My manager is exhibiting many management skills deficits.**

So instead of stating that the other person 'should not' act in a particular way, and if they do, giving them a 'label' of some kind, you accept the empirical reality of their fallibility, which helps reduce your levels of stress, and possibly anger too. Incidentally, we are not suggesting that you accept their behaviour – just their fallibility. We shall show you how to deal with unwelcome behaviour in Chapter 5.

# Activity 20
# Don't rate yourself or the other person!

The next time you hear yourself globally rate either yourself or another person, use the situation as an opportunity to quickly start rating the aspect of yourself or the other person that you dislike, and not the individual in a global manner. Note whether this helps you to reduce your stress levels, thereby enabling you to deal with the situation in a more appropriate way.

This will seem like an easy exercise to undertake. Don't be deceived. After years of regular practice of rating yourself or others, learning just to rate their behaviours or aspects of them can be a tough challenge!

# Inference chaining

Do you ever find that you feel stressed or anxious about a situation or forthcoming event but you cannot quite put your finger on the apparent cause of this unease? In extreme cases you may even choose to avoid the situation in case something bad may happen.

Recall the ABCDEF model previously described in this chapter. Inference chaining is a technique that helps you to increase your understanding about the most critical or relevant aspect of the Activating event 'A' that you may be stressed about. This is a useful technique in that it helps you to refine the problem and then assist you in eliciting the key stress-inducing thoughts (SITs) or performance-interfering thoughts (PITs). On many occasions the initial problem noted at A in the ABC model is not the real underlying issue that needs to be addressed. We mentioned in Chapter 2, Table 2.2 that an inference is an interpretation that goes beyond observable reality, but which gives meaning to it. And what's more, it may be accurate or inaccurate. In the following real case example note that the coach (SP) asks the coachee what he is most anxious about. As the coachee responded, the coach did not challenge the responses and assumes they are accurate and true. Often we don't question our inferences and that can lead to unnecessary stress.

## Case study

Jack was anxious about not giving good presentations at work. To help Jack and the coach understand what the underlying fear was about, they used inference chaining. The steps are shown below (adapted from Palmer, 2009: 11–12):

*Coach:* So the problem appears to be that you become anxious about not giving good presentations. It might be useful to discover if that is what you are really anxious about. Is it okay if we investigate this in more depth?

*Coachee:* Okay.

*Coach:* What is anxiety-provoking in your mind about not giving a good presentation?

*Coachee:* My colleagues may laugh. (NB. 1st inference)

*Coach:* Let's assume for the moment that they do laugh, what is anxiety-provoking about that?

*Coachee:* I'll be discredited. They might think I'm stupid. (NB. 2nd and 3rd inferences)

*Coach:* For the moment let's assume you are discredited and are seen as stupid, what's anxiety-provoking about that?

*Coachee:* My boss may get to hear about it and I could lose my job. (NB. 4th inference)

*Coach:* If you did lose your job, what would you be anxious about?

*Coachee:* Well, I suppose I might lose my flat and end up on the streets. (NB. 5th inference)

(NB. Coach now reviews the inferences)

*Coach:* I'd just like to review what we've covered. You

are possibly anxious about a number of issues: 1. your colleagues laughing; 2. being discredited; 3. being seen as stupid; 4. you could lose your job; 5. you could lose your flat and end up on the street... When you are getting anxious what do you think you are most anxious about?

*Coachee:* I very much doubt I'll lose my flat and end up on the street. But my job means so much to me. I wouldn't want to lose it. It's what I've always wanted.

*Coach:* Are you saying that it's not so much the presentation you're anxious about but losing the job you treasure is the real fear?

(NB. The coach has derived the hypothesised Critical 'A', in other words, most relevant aspect of the Activating event)

*Coachee:* Yeah.

The hypothesised Critical 'A' or key inference has now been found. Although this has been found the task is not quite finished yet. You can use this new data to progress onto the A–B step in the ABC model of stress. This involves eliciting the stress-inducing, performance-interfering or resilience-reducing thoughts and beliefs. The use of imagery at this step can be really helpful as can be seen below. Let's return to the example of Jack:

*Coach:* I want you to really imagine you have lost your job... The job you've always wanted. Remember, you've spent years striving to get this job and you've lost it. Can you imagine this in your mind's eye?

*Coachee:* I can.

*Coach:* What are you telling yourself at this very moment?

*Coachee:* I must not lose this job. (NB. A rigid, absolutist, demanding belief)
*Coach:* And if you did lose it?

(Question is asked to help the coachee to make conscious Jack's feared event)

*Coachee:* I couldn't stand it. Life would be awful. (NB. Low frustration tolerance and Awfulising beliefs)
Coach: How would you see yourself as a person?

(NB. Coach checks out if the coachee might lower self-acceptance if the job is lost)

*Coachee:* A total failure! (NB. Low self-acceptance)

Inference chaining is an advanced self-coaching technique and is particularly useful when you are uncertain what you are stressed about. You may want to revisit Activity 14 if you now suspect that the initial Activating event or situation you used was not the Critical 'A'.

# Summary

- **This cognitive approach to tackling stress is not new. Stoic philosophers 2,000 years ago realised that our thinking contributes to our stress levels.**
- **Emotions are difficult to create without thoughts and/or mental images in your mind's eye.**
- **There are 15 thinking errors that exacerbate stress.**
- **A range of thinking skills can be used to deal with thinking errors.**

- Stress-alleviating thoughts can be useful alternatives to stress-inducing thoughts.
- Self-esteem can create problems for us, whereas self-acceptance may be a more powerful and enduring concept.
- It is valid to rate skills and aspects of a person, but not valid to rate the person globally.
- Inference chaining can be used to discover what you really are stressed about.

Now make notes on what you have learnt.

# 4

# Changing your imagery

We have observed that people are far less likely to deal successfully with a stressful or challenging situation if they have not prepared for it. This is common sense. Just imagine giving a presentation with inadequate preparation, or not revising for an important exam! What would have been the outcome if you had not had lessons before your driving test? We suspect that you would have been very likely to fail.

Another observation worth making is that, prior to stressful events, people tend to have negative images or pictures in their mind's eye about how they are going to cope – or, to be more accurate, not going to cope – with the situation. These images of doom and gloom seldom reduce stress levels, so the person concerned gradually becomes more and more stressed prior to the event. This can even affect sleep, because the person finds it difficult to switch off at bedtime, and even if he or she does get off to sleep, it is often only to wake up early.

When stressed, staying focused on goals can be difficult. Also, we tend to comfort eat or smoke more. Fortunately, there are a number of imagery exercises that psychologists have developed to help most people deal with these problems. In the next section we shall provide six powerful methods to put you ahead of the stress game.

## Coping imagery

This is probably one of the most effective stress-management techniques to help people deal with difficult situations or potential stress scenarios, and can even assist in extreme cases such as phobias. By imagining yourself coping with the feared situation you directly challenge the negative or catastrophic imagery that may be winding you up prior to the event. Notice that we have used the word 'coping' and not 'mastering'. This is crucial, because most people have little confidence in themselves actually performing perfectly, and so have no belief in mastery imagery. Coping imagery enables you to accept that you may not be able to give that perfect presentation, be the life and soul of the party, make no errors at that important job interview, or make few mistakes when meeting your new partner's family or friends. What it does instead is use a step-by-step approach to help you deal with adversity. It is a type of rehearsal imagery that helps to build up confidence. To grasp the basic technique, give Activity 21 a go.

## Activity 21
## Coping imagery

Step 1    **Think of a future situation that you are stressed about.**
Step 2    **Note down the aspects of the situation that you are most stressed about.**
Step 3    **Develop ways to deal with these difficulties.**
Step 4    **Now carefully visualise yourself in the feared situation. Slowly picture yourself coping with each anticipated difficulty as it arises. Repeat this procedure three or four times.**

**Step 5   Practise Step 4 daily, especially when you become stressed about the forthcoming event.**

The sticking point for some people is Step 3 – they are unable to develop ways to deal with the situation. In these cases we recommend that it may be helpful to discuss the problem with an experienced colleague, friend or family member. Remember, the idea is to deal with your worst fears and not to pretend that they simply may not happen.

For example, if you are most stressed about being asked difficult questions after giving a presentation, then focus on how you would deal with this situation should it occur. Perhaps you might decide the best strategy would be to inform the audience that you are unsure of the answer to the particular question but will get back to the person after the presentation. This strategy would then become the key aspect of the visualisation to practise in Step 4. To return to the classic example that triggers stress for many people, the driving test: the visualisation at Step 4 would include seeing yourself preparing for the day, having a driving lesson beforehand, meeting the test examiner, undertaking difficult manoeuvres and so on.

This method helps to prevent negative images creating high levels of stress, and thereby becoming self-fulfilling prophecies. Many successful managers and caring parents have found that they can teach their staff and children coping imagery to deal with a range of problems. The latter find it particularly useful to calm nerves associated with examinations.

# Self-motivation imagery

Motivation imagery is used to help people inspire themselves to action in whatever area of life they need a quick jump-start. It was developed by Palmer and Neenan at the Centre for Coaching, who found that many of their clients avoided life changes because they feared they would not be able to cope with the stress created.

Motivation imagery consists, first, of visualising spending the rest of your life not doing what you want to do, and, second, visualising actually doing what you want to do. Activity 22 provides the framework for using self-motivation imagery.

# Activity 22
# Self-motivation imagery

**Spend a few minutes thinking about possible areas of your life that you could improve by taking action that you have avoided. Examples may include: changing job or going for promotion; returning to study; finishing a significant relationship; writing a book; or challenging your manager, partner, parents or in-laws about some important issue. If you are unemployed, have you become disillusioned after receiving many 'rejections'?**

**Assuming you are not too depressed about the area of life you would like to change, undertake the exercise below. Once you start, it is important to work through all three steps.**

Step 1  Visualise the rest of your life not having undertaken the change that you would like to. To assist in this exercise, imagine the effect upon yourself, and perhaps on significant others too, for the rest of your life until the day you die if you do absolutely nothing. Think of your regrets, too. Imagine the effect year by year.

Step 2  Now visualise yourself undertaking what you want to do, and then see the short- and long-term positive benefits of the change to you, and possibly others.

Step 3  Now consider how you are going to put Step 2 into action.

It is important that Step 1 (known as 'inaction' imagery) is visualised before Step 2 (known as 'action' imagery), otherwise it is possible you may demotivate yourself, which is not the intention of the exercise! Motivation imagery has helped to change people's lives and pull them out of a boring, stressful rut into a new and exciting domain.

## Staying focused (or goal) imagery

It is important when attempting to handle stress and maximise performance that you see further than the current crisis that may be occurring. Developing personal and work-related short-, medium- and long-term goals can be beneficial and help you to stay on track and move forward. Staying focused imagery also known as goal-focused imagery is a technique that will assist you to remember your goals on a daily basis (see Palmer and Puri, 2006). Activity 23 describes the process.

## Activity 23
## Staying focused or goal imagery

Step 1   Choose which area you want to work on first; either personal/social or work/career-related goals. (Alternatively, you may wish to work on a mix of both personal and work-related goals simultaneously. We have suggested just working on one area at a time as our coachees have found this easier.) Now reflect upon what you want or need to achieve in the specific area from now onwards.

Step 2   Develop realistic short-, medium- and long-term goals for your personal and/or work life. Note them down.

Step 3   For each goal develop an associated image or picture that will remind you of it. (For example, if you have a personal medium-term goal of taking up rock climbing, you may have a picture in your mind's eye of a particular rock face or mountain that you know. If you have a short-term work goal of a career change, you could picture yourself in a building that represents the new career or the college where you may undertake the retraining.)

Step 4   Now practise linking the goal with the image/picture.

Step 5   On a regular basis, use associated images or pictures in your mind's eye to remind you of your goals. You can practise this exercise at any convenient time such as when waiting for a train or bus or when relaxing in the bath.

## Time projection imagery

People often lose their perspective in relation to a stressful situation, such as becoming unemployed, failing an exam, relationship break-ups or performing poorly. Becoming stressed does not usually help them to deal with the situation in a constructive manner, and they often lose sight of their goal. Time projection imagery helps to keep the event in perspective, and so is a useful 'de-awfulising' tool. Activity 24 explains how.

## Activity 24
## Time projection imagery

Step 1   Think of a current problem or situation that you are stressed about.

Step 2   Picture yourself 3 months in the future. Will the current problem be as stressful as it is now?

Step 3   Picture yourself 6 months in the future. Will the current problem be as stressful or as important as it is now? Can you see yourself getting on with your life?

Step 4   Picture yourself 12 months in the future. Will the current problem be as stressful or as important as it is now? Can you see yourself getting on with your life?

Step 5   Picture yourself 2 years in the future. Will the current problem be as stressful or as important as it is now? Will you laugh at your problem when you look back at it? Can you see yourself having fun again?

Step 6   Picture yourself 5 years in the future. Will the memory and significance of the problem fade into the past? If you still find it difficult to imagine a positive future, picture having a new job or career, different friends, or whatever is appropriate.

## Relaxation imagery

Relaxation imagery is an excellent method to help achieve a relaxed state of body and mind. It involves picturing in your mind's eye one of your favourite relaxing places. The scene can be real or imaginary – sunbathing on a beach, walking through a park, taking a relaxing bath. Activity 25 describes the procedure.

## Activity 25
## Relaxation imagery

Step 1   Find a quiet place where you are unlikely to be disturbed. If possible, reduce the level of lighting.

Step 2    Find a comfortable position and lie down or sit quietly.

Step 3    Close your eyes and picture one of your favourite relaxing places.

Step 4    Focus on the colours in your relaxing place.

Step 5    Focus on one colour in particular.

Step 6    Focus on the sounds or silence in your relaxing place.

Step 7    Imagine touching something in your relaxing place.

Step 8    Focus on any aromas or smells in your relaxing place.

Step 9    In your own time, open your eyes.

Anyone who regularly practises this method will be able to achieve a relaxed state relatively quickly and with little effort. If you are really keen to be able to master relaxation imagery, we recommend that you practise it twice a day for 14 days. After this amount of practice you will discover that you will be able to switch into it with ease. Many of our coaching or counselling clients have learnt to use this method with their eyes open while standing on crowded city trains, but this does take practice!

## Anti-craving imagery

When we are stressed or under pressure we may comfort eat and consume our favourite snack foods; and if we are smokers, under stress we will generally increase our nicotine intake by smoking more. Starting and maintaining a healthy eating, weight-control diet or a stop-smoking programme can both be difficult tasks to undertake. Mental imagery is often central to cravings especially food cravings (see Harvey et al, 2005). As soon as you start a diet it is likely you will start to picture your favourite food or snack and if you stop smoking, you will picture the source of your nicotine such as a cigarette or cigar. You may have noticed that craving intensity increases if you start to imagine food or a cigarette. It's particularly worse for dieters. You may even start to salivate as you imagine your favourite food. Anti-craving imagery helps you deal with these images of food or other items you may crave by replacing them with neutral pictures instead. Activity 26 describes how you can practise anti-craving imagery. (This technique can be used in conjunction with other health-related interventions in Chapter 6.)

## Activity 26
## Anti-craving imagery

Step 1   Before you start your weight-control or stop-smoking programme, consider a neutral picture you could imagine easily in your mind's eye. It should not have any association with your particular craving. For example, imagine the appearance of a rainbow or green hill or forest.

Step 2   Close your eyes. Now spend 10 minutes really focusing hard on your neutral visualisation. Imagine the colours; look at the item from different angles.

Step 3   Now imagine what you crave that could undermine your weight-control or stop-smoking programme; for example, chocolate or crisps. As you start to picture the item, within two to three seconds, replace the image with your neutral image such as the brightly coloured rainbow.

Step 4   Start your programme and as soon as an item you crave literally pops into your mind, replace the image with your neutral image.

The instructions for the imagery exercises we have covered in this chapter can easily be recorded onto an audio cassette tape or iPod which can be played when you are undertaking the activities. In Chapter 6, which focuses on physical health, we include another imagery method that helps physical and mental relaxation. If you are in desperate need of relaxation, go directly to page 132 and attempt Activity 34; then go to Chapter 5 once the exercise has been completed.

## Summary

- Imagery can help you to build up confidence before an event.
- For many people, imagery techniques can be as helpful as cognitive techniques.
- Coping imagery is one of the most powerful techniques to help you to deal with future events and reduce stress.
- Rehearsal in your mind's eye of performance-related tasks can reduce stress and enhance outcomes.
- Motivation imagery can help to motivate.
- Time projection imagery can help you to de-awfulise events.
- Staying focused (or goal) imagery helps to reinforce and remind you of your goals.
- With regular practice, relaxation imagery leads to a relaxed state relatively quickly.
- Anti-craving imagery can help healthy eating, weight control and stop-smoking programmes.
- Regular practice makes it much easier to use imagery techniques and methods.

Now make notes on what you have learnt.

# 5

# Changing your behaviour

Changing your behaviour to conquer stress sounds easy enough, but it usually involves hard work. What interests psychologists about human behaviour is why people do or do not do certain things. People may have the ability to be good time managers, be assertive, and choose the right friends and colleagues for support. Yet they often decide not to apply these skills when they need them!

In this chapter we shall focus on four main behavioural areas: Type A behaviour, social support, assertion and time management. We shall also look at why we do not always use the skills we possess in stressful situations.

## What type are you, A or B?

Researchers have found that people who exhibit certain behaviours known as type behaviours are more likely to experience coronary heart disease as they age. These behaviours tend to be a response to external pressures such as deadlines and performance. Type As are often fast talking, fast eating, ambitious, impatient when waiting in queues and so on. However, other people respond to external pressures in a more relaxed manner. These 'behavioural responses' are known as Type B behaviours.

## Activity 27
## Assessing Type A and B behaviours

Circle one number for each of the statements below which best reflects the way you behave in your everyday life. For example, if you are generally always on time for meetings, for the first statement you would circle a number between 7 and 11. However, if you are not concerned about arriving late and often do so, circle a lower number on the scale, between 1 and 5.

**Table 5.1**

| | Type A & B behaviour | |
|---|---|---|
| Casual about | 1  2  3  4  5  6  7  8  9  10  11 | Never late |
| Not competitive | 1  2  3  4  5  6  7  8  9  10  11 | Very competitive |
| Good listener | 1  2  3  4  5  6  7  8  9  10  11 | Anticipates what others are going to say (nods, attempts to finish for them) |
| Never feels rushed (even under pressure) | 1  2  3  4  5  6  7  8  9  10  11 | Always rushed |
| Can wait patiently | 1  2  3  4  5  6  7  8  9  10  11 | Impatient whilst waiting |

| Takes things one at a time | 1 2 3 4 5 6 7 8 9 10 11 | Tries to do many things at once, thinks about what to do next |
|---|---|---|
| Slow, deliberate talker | 1 2 3 4 5 6 7 8 9 10 11 | Emphatic in speech, fast and forceful |
| Cares about satisfying him-/herself no matter what others may think | 1 2 3 4 5 6 7 8 9 10 11 | Wants a good job recognised by others |
| Slow doing things | 1 2 3 4 5 6 7 8 9 10 11 | Fast (eating, walking) |
| Easy going | 1 2 3 4 5 6 7 8 9 10 11 | Hard driving (pushing yourself and others) |
| Expresses feelings | 1 2 3 4 5 6 7 8 9 10 11 | Hides feelings |
| Many outside interests | 1 2 3 4 5 6 7 8 9 10 11 | Few interests outside work/ home |
| Unambitious | 1 2 3 4 5 6 7 8 9 10 11 | Ambitious |
| Casual | 1 2 3 4 5 6 7 8 9 10 11 | Eager to get things done |

Source: Cooper's adaptation of the Bortner Type A scale.

To find out your score, add up all the circled numbers above and plot the total on the scale below to see whether you exhibit Type A or Type B behaviours.

*Type B*                    *Type A*

14            84            154

The majority of people have a score near 84, generally plus or minus 20. If you scored over 84, you tend towards Type A behaviour, and if your score was under 84, then you tend towards Type B behaviour. The more Type A behaviour you exhibit, the easier it is for you to become stressed, impatient, frustrated and angry, and literally switch on the stress response, which has a physiological affect upon your body.

In reality, some of the behaviours you may have given a high score may not actually trigger frustration and anger in you. For example, some people do not find being ambitious a problem. Therefore if you want to reduce your Type A score, you could choose to modify those behaviours that trigger stress for you. You may need to apply cognitive, imagery and behavioural techniques such as modifying your internal demands, de-awfulising outcomes, anger management, relaxation, time-management skills and assertiveness training from this book in order to reduce your Type A behaviour.

## Social support

Research has highlighted the importance of social support networks that act as a buffer against stress. Assuming you have chosen the right person to speak to, work colleagues, family or friends can provide appropriate guidance and support when necessary. Activity 28, which focuses on your support networks, may reveal your strengths and weaknesses in this area.

# Activity 28
# Support networks

**Complete the Social Support Questionnaire below to
assess your support networks.**

**Table 5.2**

**Social Support Questionnaire**
**Social support: personal problems**
Think of a situation that has caused you a great deal of personal
stress. To what extent did each of the following help you with the
problem?
1 indicates little support; 5 a great deal of social support

| | | | | | |
|---|---|---|---|---|---|
| Husband/wife, partner | 1 | 2 | 3 | 4 | 5 |
| Mother | 1 | 2 | 3 | 4 | 5 |
| Father | 1 | 2 | 3 | 4 | 5 |
| Sister | 1 | 2 | 3 | 4 . | 5 |
| Brother | 1 | 2 | 3 | 4 | 5 |
| Other relative | 1 | 2 | 3 | 4 | 5 |
| Close friend | 1 | 2 | 3 | 4 | 5 |
| Casual friend | 1 | 2 | 3 | 4 | 5 |
| Work colleague | 1 | 2 | 3 | 4 | 5 |
| Doctor/clergy/therapist/coach | 1 | 2 | 3 | 4 | 5 |

Plot your total score below:

Low support                    High support
0          10          40          50

Note: a positive total score is 10, when one person is assigned 3 or
more on the scale.

Source: Cooper *et al* (1988).

**Social Support Questionnaire**
**Social support: work problems**
Think of a situation at work that has caused you a great deal of personal stress. To what extent did each of the following help you with the problem?

1 indicates little support; 5 a great deal of social support

| | | | | | |
|---|---|---|---|---|---|
| Husband/wife, partner | 1 | 2 | 3 | 4 | 5 |
| Mother | 1 | 2 | 3 | 4 | 5 |
| Father | 1 | 2 | 3 | 4 | 5 |
| Sister | 1 | 2 | 3 | 4 | 5 |
| Brother | 1 | 2 | 3 | 4 | 5 |
| Other relative | 1 | 2 | 3 | 4 | 5 |
| Close friend | 1 | 2 | 3 | 4 | 5 |
| Casual friend | 1 | 2 | 3 | 4 | 5 |
| Manager | 1 | 2 | 3 | 4 | 5 |
| Colleague | 1 | 2 | 3 | 4 | 5 |
| Subordinate | 1 | 2 | 3 | 4 | 5 |
| Doctor/clergy/therapist/coach | 1 | 2 | 3 | 4 | 5 |

Low support                              High support
0                10            40              50

Note a positive total score is 10, when one peson is assigned 3 or more on the scale.

Source: Cooper *et al* (1988).

Work problems often require somebody who is task-focused, whereas home-life difficulties often need a sympathetic ear, though it is not always this straightforward. Some people are deterred from talking to others about their problems, because they view it as a sign of weakness. They may even withdraw from supportive relationships, paradoxically at a time when they most need them. You should view discussing your problems with appropriate others as a strength, because you are then more likely to be given alternative ways to deal with the problems.

## Assertiveness training

It is very difficult to be a good time manager without assertiveness skills – hence our focus on this topic before we examine the well-known method for conquering stress: time management.

Assertive behaviour involves being able to ask for what you want, stand up for yourself, complain appropriately, defend yourself and give constructive feedback to others when necessary. With luck, its use avoids such negative consequences as exploitation, resentment, misunderstanding and passiveness.

## Activity 29
## Behaviour

**There are three types of behaviour that people tend to exhibit: aggressive, non-assertive (passive) and assertive. Tick the ones that you recognise in yourself.**

### Aggressive

**Behaviour:**
- **finger pointing;**
- **leaning forward;**
- **sharp, sarcastic or firm voice;**
- **fist(s) thumping;**
- **loud voice/shouting;**
- **violation of others' rights;**
- **dominating demeanour.**

**Phrases/words used:**
- You'd better ...
- It's your fault!
- You're joking!
- You ought/must/should ...
- Don't be stupid!

## Non-assertive/passive

**Behaviour:**
- shrugging;
- hunched shoulders;
- whining, quiet or giggly voice;
- hand wringing;
- shifting of body weight;
- stepping backward;
- downcast eyes.

**Phrases/words used:**
- maybe;
- perhaps;
- just;
- only;
- I wonder if you could ...
- I'm hopeless/useless.
- I can't.
- Never mind.
- It's not important.
- I mean ...
- Well, uh ... .

## Assertive

**Behaviour:**
- relaxed demeanour;
- lack of hostility;

- smiling when pleased;
- no fidgeting/slouching;
- collaborative approach;
- good eye contact.

**Phrases/words used:**
- cooperative: let's, we could ...
- open questions: What do you think/want? How do you feel?
- 'I' statements: I think, I want, I fear, I feel ...

In Activity 29 the type of behaviour you tend to exhibit to others is indicated by the section in which you have the most ticks. We recommend that the aggressive and the non-assertive or passive behaviours are reduced and the assertive behaviours increased in any social interaction, thereby creating a win–win philosophy, as opposed to the more common win–lose. Being aggressive tends to wind up others as well as the person concerned, leading to conflict and resentment.

Passive behaviour is tantamount to letting others 'walk all over you', which tends to lead to reduced self-esteem and depression. It is worth noting that some people exhibit a passive-aggressive combination by having aggressive body behaviour but using passive language instead. They tend to be manipulative, sarcastic and cynical, although they may avoid direct conflict.

## Assertiveness rights

The literature on assertion usually recognises a number of assertiveness rights. Do you agree that you have the right to:

- say no?
- consider your needs important?
- make mistakes?
- take responsibility for your behaviour?

- express your feelings in an appropriate manner without violating anybody else's rights?
- set your own priorities?
- be understood?
- be you?
- be assertive without feeling guilty?
- respect yourself?

If you disagree with any of these assertiveness rights, discuss the particular 'right' with a trusted friend or colleague and obtain his or her views.

# Assertiveness skills

There are a number of assertiveness skills you may wish to attempt at the next appropriate opportunity. We outline the key skills under the following headings.

## Workable compromise

You offer the other person(s) a compromise, assuming that your self-worth or self-respect is not being challenged. For example:

Your manager: We are getting desperately behind. Can you come in on Saturday morning and finish the paperwork? You: I've agreed to take my daughter horse-riding tomorrow morning, and I'm not prepared to let her down. However, I can start work earlier next Monday and do my best to get the work finished. Is that OK?

## Negative enquiry

Instead of receiving just global, negative feedback, negative enquiry encourages the other person to provide specific information about your behaviour in a more constructive manner. For example:

Relative: You are a totally hopeless parent!
You: Can you share with me in what way I am hopeless?

## Broken record

This involves stating your viewpoint in a relaxed manner while ignoring irrelevant logic or arguments, manipulative traps and/or baiting. For example:

Student: You are being really unfair. Why should my results suffer just because my project came in late?
Tutor: Unfortunately, the regulations state that a project has to be submitted on the due date; otherwise marks are taken off.
Student: You've never liked me from the start of the course. I bet you let others off.
Tutor: The regulations apply to everybody. Marks are taken off if a project is submitted late.

## Fogging

By simply acknowledging your mistakes, this skill helps when others are using 'put-downs' or manipulative criticism. This helps you to maintain your self-respect. For example:

Manager: Late again! You're letting the office down.
You: Three months ago I was late when the train broke down, and unfortunately it happened again today.

## The three-step model of assertion

The three-step model can be used in any situation, but is of particular use when you feel under pressure to comply with other people's demands. Using this model you can make your point in an assertive manner, without being offensive, and still remain focused on your wishes, without becoming emotional. Palmer and Puri (2006: 66) describe the model as follows:

**Step 1:** Actively listen to what the other person is saying, and demonstrate to the other individual that you have heard and understood what he or she has said.
**Step 2:** Say what you think and feel. (A good linking word to use here, between Steps 1 and 2, is 'however'.)
**Step 3:** Say what you want to happen. (A good linking word to use between Steps 2 and 3 is 'and'.)

A real example illustrating the three-step model is below:

**Step 1:**    It would be nice to go out this evening.
**Step 2:**    However, I need to prepare for my work tomorrow.
**Step 3:**    And so I think I'll stay in on this occasion.

These examples show how assertiveness skills can be applied to a range of situations. Many people have the skills but choose not to use them for a variety of reasons, including fear of upsetting others because they are 'people pleasers', having low self-worth and so usually putting others' wants first, or having a desire for others to like them. If you recognise one or more of these issues, you may wish to return to Chapter 3 and examine the thinking errors you are possibly making.

There is a caveat: assertiveness skills are not always recommended, because their use by some people can increase the likelihood of violence occurring, or because an employer may use their being deployed as an excuse to dismiss the person. In these situations an alternative course of action may be necessary.

# Time management

If you can manage your time successfully, you are more likely to control or conquer the majority of your stress at home and at work. Now that we have considered thinking skills (in Chapter 3) and how to be assertive (in this chapter), time management should become easier to use on a daily basis. However, we need first of all to consider why people procrastinate.

## Activity 30
## Do you procrastinate?

Think back to the last time you had an important project to complete, essay to write, exam to study for or presentation to give. Did you waste any time doing any of the items listed below? Tick the behaviours you performed:

- cleaning and tidying your desk;
- dusting or tidying your room or computer screen;
- cleaning the kitchen floor;
- washing the windows;
- cutting the grass;
- weeding the garden;
- cleaning the car;
- talking to distant relatives;
- deleting unwanted e-mails;
- responding to unimportant e-mails;
- tidying up computer folders;
- surfing the internet;
- playing computer games;
- spending an inordinate amount of time making a priority list;
- spending days preparing for the work by obtaining yet more background information;

- tidying the filing system;
- doing the unimportant jobs in the in-tray;
- answering unnecessary telephone calls;
- consuming more drinks, food or cigarettes than usual;
- whinging to colleagues about the amount of work you have;
- blaming your boss or others;
- telling others that you work best at the eleventh hour (or even later!).

So why do many people under pressure procrastinate? Look at the graph in Figure 5.1. As soon as a person has to do something he or she wants to do well at, his or her stress levels often increase. However, when people start cleaning the floor, doing the unimportant things in the in-tray, deleting e-mails or whatever, their stress levels temporarily drop. Yet, some time later when they finish procrastinating and think about the job in hand, their stress levels rise even higher than before as they realise they have wasted valuable time.

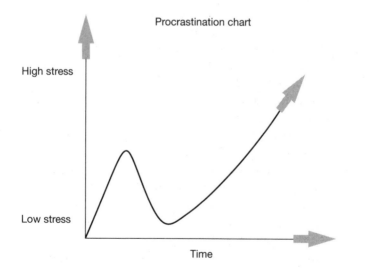

Source: Cooper and Palmer (2000).

**Figure 5.1** Procrastination chart

The key is to recognise initially that you are procrastinating – in other words, doing something that is not directly focused on helping you to achieve your goal. If you also recognise a thinking error such as labelling (for instance, 'If I fail my exams, I'll be a failure'), then challenge it (see Chapter 3).

Sometimes people procrastinate for another reason: there is a boring task they need to do, such as completing their annual tax return. In these cases the thinking error is generally, 'I can't stand doing boring jobs.' Therefore the 'I can't-stand-it-itis' should be challenged (see Chapter 3).

See procrastination as the thief of time. On your deathbed you are unlikely to say, 'I should have spent more time procrastinating!'

## Top tips for the time manager

- At the beginning of the week, make a list of your goals and targets, and prioritise. Revise the list daily, as necessary. Refer regularly to the list.
- Spend only an appropriate amount of time planning your workload or project.
- Avoid procrastinating. Challenge the thinking errors or beliefs that underpin this behaviour.
- To avoid making errors, do one task at a time.
- Allow time for the unexpected, and be realistic about how much work you and your colleagues can do.
- Avoid automatically saying yes to others' requests. With time-consuming projects, ask yourself whether you really need to agree to the request being asked. Use assertiveness skills; say no when necessary.
- When possible, deal with incoming postal mail or e-mails as soon as you open them, or if under pressure, consider prioritising them and dealing with the unimportant mail later.

- Group outgoing telephone calls. List items to be discussed and be precise.
- Prepare for meetings and list items you wish to discuss.

# Developing goals

Research has found that developing goals helps a person to enhance motivation and remain focused on projects or particular issues that need addressing which can be personal and/or work-related (Locke, 1996; Locke and Latham, 1990). The development of goals is an important aspect of stress, time, and life management. Being goal-less, especially at work is likely to lead to underachievement.

Goals can be specific such as 'losing three kilos by my next birthday' or less specific such as 'losing weight'. The specific goal in our example is time bounded and assuming it is realistic, will generally help the person to work hard at achieving the goal. However, a vague goal of just 'losing weight' is less likely to assist a person to remain focused on the task. It's hard to monitor and evaluate achievement and success when no specific target has been considered. Ongoing feedback as a person works towards achieving a goal can be beneficial. Another factor worth considering when developing goals if you want to remain motivated is to ensure they are challenging but within your capabilities.

A helpful acronym to assist in goal development is SMART. The case study below highlights its application (taken from Palmer, 2007a).

## Case study: SMART

In the workplace a fair percentage of employees get stressed and anxious about giving presentations to their peers or to senior management. In this example, the employee, Frank, copes by avoiding giving presentations instead of using them as an opportunity to improve his skills. Once his Director suggested that he 'should brush up on presentations', he became more motivated to tackle the problem. Developing SMART goals helped this process. Normally a good idea to take ownership of the goal is by prefixing it with 'I want...':

| | | |
|---|---|---|
| S | = Specific (Simple and Stretching): | I want to improve my work presentations by summer in time for the company conference in London. |
| M | = Measurable (and can be Monitored): | I could use evaluation feedback forms to measure clarity, speed of delivery etc. |
| A | = Achievable (Agreed, Attractive): | Yes it is achievable. However, from now on I should give presentations instead of avoiding them so I can improve my skills. |
| R | = Realistic: | I can achieve this goal. I'm totally committed to this especially since the Director suggested that I should brush up on my presentations! |
| T | = Timescale (or Timebound): | There are weekly opportunities to give presentations over the next three months. This will give me sufficient time to hone my skills. |

As you work through this book, when you need to develop goals, consider noting them down in the SMART format. Also you may find it useful to use goal-focused imagery technique to remind you of your goals (see page 95).

## Summary

- Aggressive or hostile Type A behaviour can have a negative health impact on both individuals and their colleagues and family.
- Social support is an excellent buffer against stress.
- Assertion skills are essential for managing stress, especially if you want to become a good time manager.
- Assertion skills need regular practice.
- The application of time-management skills can really help to prevent stress.
- Procrastinating often reduces stress in the short-term, but a negative stress pay-off comes later.
- Developing goals is an important aspect of stress, time and life management.

Now make notes on what you have learnt.

# 6

# Improving your physical health to help you conquer stress

There are a number of key strategies you can undertake to help deal with your physiological response to stress. In this chapter we shall focus on exercise, nutrition and physiological relaxation methods. The short self-assessment questionnaire in Activity 31 will indicate whether this chapter is for you, or whether you might be better off proceeding directly to Chapter 7.

## Activity 31
## Healthy Living Questionnaire

**For each of the questions below, focus on the answer that most closely relates to you. The key is:**

1. = Never
2. = Rarely
3. = Periodically
4. = Regularly
5. = Very often

## Exercise scale

1. Do you do any physical exercise, such as walking, cycling or jogging?
2. Do you take part in any sports activities that involve exerting yourself physically?
3. Do you feel exhausted after physically exerting yourself a little?
4. How often is exercise part of your daily routine?

## Nutrition scale

5. How often do you drink more than five cups of tea a day?
6. How often do you drink more than five cups of coffee a day?
7. How often do you eat three meals a day?
8. How often do you eat between meals?
9. How often do you eat fruit and vegetables?
10. How often do you eat foods high in saturated fats?
11. How often do you binge-drink alcohol?

## Miscellaneous scale

12. Are you under- or over-weight? Yes/No
13. Do you drink more than the recommended weekly guidelines of alcohol (14 units for women and 21 units for men)? Yes/No
14. Do you smoke? Yes/No

Below are the desirable answers:

1. 4 or 5
2. 4 or 5
3. 1 or 2 (consider checking with your GP if you have any other result)
4. 4 or 5

5. 1 or 2 (NB 3 cups a day is beneficial.)
6. 1 or 2
7. 4 or 5
8. 1 or 2
9. 4 or 5
10. 1 or 2
11. 1 or 2
12. No
13. No
14. Preferably no (if yes, rarely!).

Depending upon how you scored on this questionnaire, you may wish to increase or decrease certain behaviours or activities. If you answered any question with an undesirable response, you may wish to focus on that area of your life. This chapter will cover most of the relevant topics.

## Alcohol

Alcohol depresses the central nervous system. Depending on the amount consumed, the short-term effects can include relaxation, slurred speech, reduced motor coordination and cognitive ability, mild euphoria and disturbed sleep. An excess of alcohol can lead to nausea, vomiting, coma or even death. The long-term effects of drinking high levels of alcohol include liver disease, heart disease, hypertension, impaired functioning of the brain, cirrhosis and intestinal bleeding. Research has shown that the consumption of alcohol in moderation is fine, and a couple of units of wine per day can actually be beneficial, because alcohol makes the blood less sticky, thus reducing your likelihood to suffer from blood clots or strokes.

Health professionals recommend that the maximum consumption of alcohol is 21 units a week for adult males and 14 units a week for adult females. One unit is a glass of wine or half a pint of beer. If you now realise that you are drinking heavily or just want to reduce your alcohol intake, keeping a drinking diary to monitor your intake really helps. Another useful tip is to purchase non-alcoholic alternatives and drink these when you would normally have alcohol. For example, have a glass of grape juice rather than a glass of wine.

Below is a drinking diary you could use to monitor your consumption.

**Table 6.1** Drinking diary

| Date | Beverage | When/where/with whom | Units | Total |
|------|----------|----------------------|-------|-------|
|      |          |                      |       |       |
|      |          |                      |       |       |
|      |          |                      |       |       |
|      |          |                      |       |       |
|      |          |                      |       |       |
|      |          |                      |       |       |
|      |          |                      |       |       |
|      |          |                      |       |       |
|      |          |                      |       |       |
|      |          |                      |       |       |

Weekly total =

## Units (a rough guide)

| | |
|---|---|
| Wine (11% alcohol content) | standard glass = 1 unit |
| Ordinary strength beer, lager, cider | half pint = 1 unit; 1 pint = 2 units |
| Strong beer, lager, cider | half pint = 2 units; 1 pint = 4 units |
| Sherry | standard small measure = 1 unit |
| Spirits | standard English measure = 1 unit |

# Caffeine

Unlike alcohol, caffeine is a stimulant to the central nervous system. It is found in tea, coffee, various soft drinks and other food products. It has an uplifting effect, although in excess its consumption can lead to feelings of anxiety, palpitations, increased nervousness and alertness, restlessness and insomnia. People with a high intake of caffeine generally benefit from reducing the amount of caffeine they consume. However, it is recommended that the reduction is gradual because sudden cessation can cause nausea, headaches and craving for the first 36 to 48 hours. The average daily intake of caffeine in the UK is about 444 mg.

# Activity 32
# How much caffeine do you consume per day?

**Look at Table 6.2. Now work out how much caffeine you consumed yesterday. If yesterday was not a typical day, then repeat the exercise for a more typical day.**

**Table 6.2**

| Dietary source | Average caffeine concentration in 5 oz cup or weight |
| --- | --- |
| | (mg) |
| Real coffee | 100 |
| Instant coffee | 70 |
| Tea | 40 |
| Cola drink | 20 |
| Small milk chocolate bar | 20 |
| Chocolate drink | 10 |
| Decaffeinated coffee | 3 |

If you want to reduce your intake, do it gradually over a week.

Source: Parrott (1991: 210).

# Exercise

There are many benefits from taking exercise. These include improving your physical and mental health, stress busting, anger control, weight control, reducing depression and enhancing your self-esteem. For many people, exercise works by distracting them from their difficulties and problems, especially if it involves team games.

However, before you decide to take up some form of vigorous exercise such as jogging or playing squash, please note the following. If you are over 35, pregnant, convalescing or overweight, or you have asthma, bronchitis, high blood pressure (hypertension), chest pains, diabetes or a family history of heart disease, it is imperative that initially you seek advice from your medical practitioner.

## Exercise pointers

- Avoid overdoing it! Grade your training programme into manageable chunks. Avoid setting yourself difficult goals. If you feel nauseous, dizzy or in pain, stop exercising immediately.
- If your training programme is enjoyable, you are more likely to maintain it over a period of time. Perhaps exercise with family, colleagues or friends – but avoid being competitive!
- Warm up with gentle bends and stretches before you start your training programme.
- Allow for a cool-down period after exercise. Walk slowly for a few minutes.
- Choose a range of exercises, some of which are not weather-dependent.
- When using exercise equipment, you can listen to your favourite music or radio programmes to avoid boredom.
- It is not advisable to undertake arduous exercise within one or two hours of eating a heavy meal.
- Choose sports facilities that are easily accessible from your home or work.
- Integrate exercise into your everyday routine. At work use the stairs instead of the lift or escalator.

Don't give up your training programme just because you have missed it for a few days or weeks owing to work or home pressures. Use the thinking skills discussed in Chapter 3 to challenge your exercise-interfering beliefs.

# Nutrition

Why should we be careful about our diet? Poor nutrition that is lacking in the essential vitamins and minerals but includes saturated fats can lead to a range of serious disorders such as heart disease. Although a busy lifestyle can interfere with our eating habits, a healthy, balanced diet should be a goal to achieve whenever possible. In this section we focus on food to eat and food to avoid.

## Heart disease and fats

A diet rich in saturated fats increases the risk of heart disease because fatty deposits (known as blood cholesterol or low-density lipoproteins, LDLs) adhere to the arterial walls, which can lead to narrowed and eventually blocked arteries. This raises blood pressure and may finally result in a heart attack. Not all fats are potentially dangerous; therefore we shall describe the main ones below.

### Saturated fats

A number of products contain the sorts of saturated fat that can lead to heart disease, including cheese, milk, lard, hard margarine and butter. The fatty sections of pork, lamb and beef also contain high levels of saturated fats.

### Mono-unsaturated fats

Although classed as fats, the mono-unsaturated fats do not increase blood cholesterol levels, or the sticky, low-density lipoproteins. The main sources of these fats are olive oil and avocado pears. Some research has indicated that olive oil may be one of the key factors responsible for the low rate of heart disease found among Mediterranean people. Olive oil is now included in some margarines.

### Polyunsaturated fats

Polyunsaturated fats are found in such oily fish as pilchards, mackerel and sardines. Their main benefit is that they help to prevent blood clots from forming and reduce blood cholesterol levels. Another type of polyunsaturated fat is found in vegetable oils, such as soya, sunflower, corn and safflower. Some margarines are labelled 'high in polyunsaturates', and are to be preferred to butter or lard.

## Trans fats

Trans fats are a partially hydrogenated vegetable fat used in baked, fried and fast foods which can lead to heart and arterial diseases. Most food manufacturers currently do not include them on the list of contents. However, wherever possible we recommend that they are avoided. These commercially made fats are banned in Denmark.

Foods to cut down on are:

- **Fried food.**
- **Meat products such as burgers, pâtés, pork scratchings, sausages and meat with fatty portions.**
- **Canned fruit in syrup.**
- **Full-fat cheeses such as cheddar or stilton.**
- **Biscuits, white bread and sweetened breakfast cereals.**
- **Whole milk, cream and yogurt (except for low-fat natural yogurt).**
- **Products with a high sugar content, such as chocolate, sweetened fruit juices, instant custard and some cola drinks.**
- **Salt or products with a high salt content. Consult your medical practitioner initially, if you have low blood pressure.**
- **Mayonnaise and salad dressings that are oily and low in polyunsaturates or olive oil.**

Preferred foods are:

- **Poached, steamed or grilled food.**
- **Fish, poultry or lean meat. Oily fish is particularly healthy.**

- Fruit, such as apples, bananas, grapes, oranges, or fruit in natural juices.
- Low-fat cheese, cottage cheese or alternatives made with sunflower oil.
- High-fibre products that aid the digestion, including beans, bran, wholegrain bread, brown rice, cereals, pasta and oats.
- Semi-skimmed or skimmed milk.
- Mayonnaise alternatives or salad dressings low in fat or high in polyunsaturates.

## Plant sterols

Plant sterols have been clinically proven to lower the 'bad' LDL cholesterol levels by reducing the amount of cholesterol entering the bloodstream from the gut. Plant sterols are natural substances, and can be found in foods such as nuts, beans, vegetables, fruit and vegetable oils. They are now available in some margarine spreads, drinks and yogurts. Plant sterols are also available in tablet form. It is recommended that no more than 3 g of plant sterols are consumed per day, as extra amounts do not provide any additional benefits.

## Interesting research

Although we would not encourage you to drink large quantities of tea, research has found that drinking between two and five cups a day reduces the risk of strokes. Somewhat surprisingly, dark chocolate helps to lower cholesterol levels. One or two units of alcohol a day reduces the stickiness of blood, making it less likely to clot and cause a thrombosis. Because these are easy health-related changes to instigate, you may wish to consider adding them to your review at the end of this chapter.

# Weight control

Most diets do not work. Dieters temporarily reduce weight and then put it back on again. The key to controlling body weight is to understand a simple equation:

Body weight is increased when energy intake exceeds energy used.

It is that simple. But deceptively simple! If you are overweight, unless you want a medical intervention, to achieve the desired weight for your height you will need to reduce your calorific input by eating less food and expending more energy by increasing your lifestyle activity and undertaking more exercise. Once achieved, the desired weight can be maintained by keeping a correct balance between calories consumed and energy expended. Basically, it is that simple!

Lifestyle changes that help this process include avoiding snacks between meals, cutting out from your diet foods high in fats and sugars, and incorporating exercise into your daily routine, such as walking or cycling to work or to the shops, and taking part in sports such as tennis or badminton. (Bear in mind, however, that building up muscles can lead to weight gain.)

Obesity should be taken seriously, because it can lead to heart disease, stroke, high blood pressure, gallstones, arthritis, diabetes and bronchitis. It really is worth bothering about.

# Activity 33
# Weight reduction

**Do you want to lose weight? If you do, then complete the form below. It will help you to consider the key issues and examine what possible changes you may need to make to your lifestyle. It will also help you to focus on the advantages of losing weight.**

**Table 6.3**

Weight reduction and control form

For breakfast I usually eat _____

For lunch I usually eat _____

For dinner I usually eat _____

In between meals I usually eat _____

Circle answers that apply to you:

I regularly eat crisps/biscuits/sweets/pastries/pies/fried food

I regularly eat fibre-rich food such as pasta/wholemeal bread/jacket potatoes/high-fibre cereals

I, or members of my family, have suffered from stroke/diabetes/heart disease/high blood pressure

My weekly consumption of alcohol is _____ units

My sugar intake is low/medium/high

My lifestyle is sedentary/active/very active

Comments and possible changes:

_____

_____

_____

I wish to lose weight because:

_____

_____

_____

© Stephen Palmer, 1988.

If you suffer from cravings for particular food products when on a weight reduction programme, anti-craving imagery may be helpful in reducing the cravings (see page 98).

# Smoking

Regular smoking of tobacco over years is responsible for heart disease and a variety of cancers. In addition to the nicotine and tar found in cigarettes, cigarette smoke consists of about 2,000 different chemicals. Smoking is an addiction and habit-forming, therefore stopping smoking is not easy for many people. We recommend joining stop smoking groups, hypnosis, or if you experience great difficulty, cognitive behaviour therapy. In addition, many people have found nicotine patches a very useful aid. If you encounter difficulty in stopping smoking, go back to Chapter 3 and note down any thinking errors you may be using that hinder you. For example:

- **It will be too difficult to stop smoking.**
- **I'll be impossible to work or live with.**
- **I'll put on weight.**
- **I feel on edge when I'm not smoking.**
- **I can't stand feeling on edge.**
- **I don't like saying 'no' if a friend offers me a cigarette.**

You can use the thinking skills in Chapter 3 to assist you in dealing with these health-inhibiting thoughts (HITs). Create your own health-enhancing thoughts (HETs) such as:

- **Yes, it is difficult to stop smoking, but I will give it a go.**
- **I will be difficult to work or live with for a few days but I'll get over it. I'll let everybody know that.**

You may find anti-craving imagery helpful too (see page 98).

# Relaxation

There are a number of different relaxation techniques that help to reduce the physical effects of stress and tension. If you already use yoga, massage, meditation or imagery exercises successfully, you may not need to read this section.

We provide here a couple of methods that many tens of thousands of people have found useful. The methods work by helping the person to switch off mentally, thereby enhancing the parasympathetic nervous system, which aids relaxation, and the digestive and immune systems. Interestingly, research has shown that meditative techniques can lead to 50 per cent fewer visits to hospital as either an in- or out-patient. If at any time when you are using these techniques you do not like the sensation of relaxation, open your eyes and the feelings will quickly pass.

## Benson relaxation technique

This Western form of meditation was developed by H Benson, who found that it could reduce blood pressure and hypertension. A number of your choice is used as a mantra, which helps to block out unwanted thoughts. What follows here is a modified version that the authors have found helpful.

# Activity 34
# Benson relaxation technique

Step 1   If possible, find a noise-free place and reduce the level of lighting. Ensure that you will not be disturbed.

Step 2   Find a comfortable position and lie down or sit quietly.

Step 3   Close your eyes.

Step 4   Relax your muscles in groups. Start at your face and progress down to your toes.

Step 5   Focus on your breathing. Breathe naturally in through your nose and out through your mouth. Notice how your stomach may rise and fall as you breathe in and out. Avoid letting your shoulders rise as you breathe.

Step 6   In your mind, say a number such as 'one' every
time you breathe out.
Step 7   Continue for five to 20 minutes.
Step 8   Finish in your own time.

A golden rule of relaxation is not to try hard. With regular
practice it will come naturally, but like any new skill, it may take
several attempts. If you are keen to learn more about relaxation
techniques, meditation or yoga, contact your local adult
education college or obtain a good relaxation audiotape from a
reputable dealer.

## Multimodal relaxation technique

The multimodal relaxation method was developed by Professor
Stephen Palmer at the Centre for Stress Management to help
clients attending counselling and coaching sessions, and
delegates on stress management workshops to find the particular
relaxation technique that suits them. It contains a number of
different strategies including breathing, simple mantras (the
number 'one' or another number of your choice), imagery/
visualisation, sounds, smell and touch (Palmer, 1993). Once you
have given the method a go, decide which approach you prefer
for future use. Or just continue using all the techniques.

# Activity 35
# Using the multimodal relaxation
# method

Below is the multimodal relaxation method text that you
can ask someone to read to you, or record yourself
reading so you can play it back later or just read out aloud
to yourself.
    You have the choice of using the word 'you'

throughout, or changing it to 'I' if you are more comfortable using the first person singular when reading it out to yourself. Obviously, do not read out aloud the instructions to pause! If you wear contact lenses, either remove them before the exercise or do not look upwards. (NB A 'long pause' is 10 seconds.)

Begin by sitting comfortably on a chair and close your eyes. If at any time during the exercise you feel any odd feelings such as tingling sensations, light-headedness, or whatever, this is quite normal. If you open your eyes then these feelings will go away. If you carry on with the exercise, usually these feelings will disappear anyway. If you would like to, listen to the noises outside the room first of all.
Long pause
And now listen to the noises inside the room.
Pause
You may be aware of yourself breathing.
These noises will come and go throughout this session and you can choose to let them just drift over your mind or ignore them if you wish.
Pause
Now keeping your eyelids closed and without moving your head, I would like you to look upwards. Your eyes closed, just look upwards.
Long pause
Notice the feeling of tiredness.
Pause
And relaxation.
Pause
In your eye muscles.
Pause
Now let your eyes drop back down.
Pause
Notice the tiredness and relaxation in those muscles of your eyes.

Pause

Let the feeling now travel down your face to your jaw. Just relax your jaw.

Long pause

Now relax your tongue.

Pause

Let the feeling of relaxation slowly travel up over your face to the top of your head.

Pause

To the back of your head.

Long pause

Then slowly down through your neck muscles.

Pause

And down to your shoulders.

Long pause

Now concentrate on relaxing your shoulders. Just let them drop down.

Pause

Now let that feeling of relaxation now in your shoulders slowly travel down your right arm, down through the muscles, down through your elbow, down through your wrist, to your hand, right down to your finger tips.

Long pause

Let the feeling of relaxation now in your shoulders slowly travel down your left arm, down through your muscles, down through your elbow, through your wrist, down to your hand, right down to your finger tips.

Long pause

And let that feeling of relaxation now in your shoulders slowly travel down your chest right down to your stomach.

Pause

Just concentrate on your breathing.

Pause

Notice that every time you breathe out you feel more ...

Pause

... and more relaxed.

Long pause
Let the feeling of relaxation travel down from your shoulders right down your back.
Long pause
Right down your right leg, down through the muscles, through your knee, down through your ankle.
Pause
To your foot, right down to your toes.
Long pause
Let the feeling of relaxation now travel down your left leg.
Pause
Down through the muscles, down through your knee, down through your ankle.
Pause
To your foot, right down to your toes.
Long pause
I'll give you a few moments now ...
Pause
... to allow you to concentrate on any part of your body that you would like to relax further.
15 second pause minimum
I want you to concentrate on your breathing again.
Pause
Notice as you breathe ...
Pause
... on each out-breath you feel more and more relaxed.
Long pause
I would like you in your mind to say a number of your choice such as the number one.
Pause (Note: if the number one evokes an emotion in you, choose another number.)
And say it every time you breathe out.
Long pause
This will help you to push away any unwanted thoughts you may have.
Pause

Each time you breathe out just say the number in your mind.

30 second pause

I want you now ...

Pause

... to think of your favourite relaxing place.

Long pause

Imagine seeing it in your mind's eye.

Long pause

Look at the colours.

Pause

Now focus on one colour.

Pause

Now concentrate on any sounds or noises in your favourite relaxing place. If there are no sounds, then focus on the silence.

Long pause

Now concentrate on any smells or aromas in your favourite relaxing place.

Long pause

Now just imagine touching something ...

Pause

... in your favourite relaxing place.

Long pause

Just imagine how it feels.

Long pause

I want you now to concentrate on your breathing again.

Pause

Notice once again that every time you breathe out ...

Pause

... you feel more ...

Pause

... and more relaxed.

Long pause

Whenever you want to in the future, you will be able to remember your favourite place or the breathing exercise and it will help you to relax quickly.

Long pause
In a few moments' time, but not quite yet, I'm going to count to
three ...
Pause
... and you will be able to open your eyes in your own time.
Pause (Note: or insert, 'go off to sleep', if you so wish.)
One
Pause
Two
Pause
Three
Pause
Open your eyes in your own time.

© Stephen Palmer (1993).

In our experience, we have found this multimodal method of relaxation to be particularly useful for people suffering from anxiety, tension headaches, high blood pressure, insomnia, Type A behaviour, and to control the general irritability experienced by someone on a stop-smoking programme. However, care should be taken if you suffer from asthma, epilepsy or panic attacks, because relaxation can exacerbate or trigger these conditions in rare cases.

If you are interested in finding out more about relaxation, yoga or meditation, you might like to contact your local adult education service which may run classes. Alternatively, a local sports centre may run classes.

# Summary

- **Poor nutrition that is lacking in the essential vitamins and minerals but includes saturated fats can lead to a range of serious disorders such as heart disease.**

- A diet rich in saturated and trans fats increases the risk of heart disease.
- The key to controlling body weight is to understand a simple equation:

Body weight is increased when energy intake exceeds energy used.

- Relaxation can help you to lower blood pressure and become physiologically relaxed.
- A golden rule of relaxation is not to try hard.
- Relaxation skills improve with regular practice.

Now make notes on what you have learnt.

# 7

# Dealing with work-related stress

In this chapter we consider work-related stress, and how it can be tackled at both the organisational and individual levels. This will be of interest to you if you are an employee, manager, supervisor, health and safety practitioner or employer.

With the increasing recognition that employers should act to ameliorate or prevent work-related stress, and with the increasing stress litigation, there will be a greater demand upon organisations to set up stress prevention and stress management programmes.

Do you recognise any of the following symptoms at work:

- **low morale?**
- **industrial relations difficulties?**
- **high absenteeism?**
- **increase in long-term illness?**
- **increased or high turnover of staff?**
- **increased litigation?**
- **reduced efficiency?**
- **poor performance in tasks?**
- **poor quality control?**

- deadlines not being reached?
- increased bullying?
- increase in accidents?
- long-hours culture?

If you recognise more than a couple of the above symptoms, your organisation should seriously consider taking steps to deal with stress.

It is worth noting that during periods of recession some of the symptoms may be exacerbated or reduced. In addition, research has found that employees report higher levels of stress as they become more anxious about income, workload and job insecurity (see CMHA, 2009).

# Definition of stress

Although many definitions of stress exist, we recommend that in the United Kingdom we use the Health and Safety Executive (HSE) definition:

> The adverse reaction people have to excessive pressures or other types of demand placed on them.

Notice that this definition focuses on external stressors or hazards in the workplace. It complements the cognitive definition of stress we gave you in Chapter 1 in that both excessive external pressures and self-induced internal pressures we place upon ourselves can trigger stress.

# The financial and health impact of work-related stress

Two studies highlight the financial and health impact of work-related stress on the employer and employee. In 2000 the International Labour Organisation Report found that the annual financial cost of stress to the United Kingdom was £5.3 billion. The HSE now estimates that the cost has since risen to about £9.6 billion. The Whitehall II Study found associations between these hazards, health and behaviour:

- **High job demands – poor mental health, poor health functioning (ie physical health/social functioning).**
- **High effort and low reward – alcohol dependence, poor mental health, poor health functioning, sickness absence (eight days or more per year).**
- **Low social support at work – increased sickness absence, poor mental health, poor health functioning.**

To illustrate how the hazards can sometimes lead to stress and eventual breakdown, the HSE (2006b) has provided a real case example. As you will see, it really highlights why stress recognition and prevention are both very important.

## Case study: stress, mental health and rehabilitation – one man's story

I write this brief personal case study as a health and safety practitioner, in the hope that it may be of interest to others.

I had my first breakdown in 1997 (when I was 37), and my second two years later in 1999. Up until then my life had been relatively uneventful, more or less ordinary. It had followed a familiar pattern: school, university, further qualifications, kept fairly fit, healthy, hobbies, cycling, drama, writing, got married, had children, grandparents died. My life was normal – at least, as normal as life ever is.

The first time, it built up slowly, over a few months. Some of the events leading up to the breakdown are interesting, and were significant for me. But they wouldn't necessarily be significant to anyone else. As well as relationship issues at home, factors included the constant pressure to meet deadlines, and lunch only being a hurried sandwich at the desk. On one occasion, I took what most would regard as a 'minor conflict' with a senior manager at work (over a stress research project, no less!) as a major personal insult, and this blew the lid off everything for me.

It was May 1997, the day the IRA brought the country to a standstill with bomb hoaxes, just before the election. From then on life began to race wildly. I was on a high. My behaviour began to change. Gradually, more people realised that there was something wrong. At first, as far as I was concerned, I was having one of the best times of my life – I had so much creative energy. Ideas would come flooding in and I wanted to do everything, all at once. I was experiencing mania, and later delusions, as the ideas became further removed from reality, and towards the end they were profoundly disturbing. This all took place over the space of six to eight weeks. During the last few days I really wasn't making sense. I met with my manager and his boss in a relaxed environment outside of work, and they diplomatically recommended (based on my erratic and unusual behaviour over the preceding weeks) that I rest and see a doctor. By this time they had realised something was seriously wrong. Confused, at the doctors, I was recommended for psychiatric care and, on being admitted I broke down completely: I had experienced 'an acute psychotic episode'.

There were various further diagnoses: bipolar affective disorder (manic depression), stress-related illness, schizo-affective disorder, to name but a few. The symptoms were mixed, unclear. I began to recover in hospital during my first week, with medication. Medication! *One Flew Over the Cuckoo's Nest* had put me off 'medication' for life! I was in hospital for a month, and off work for three months altogether. During that time even the first, brief visit by a very caring personnel officer, on neutral ground (a coffee shop near home – even the thought of a journey into London upset me), had me in tears for no reason. Everybody was very supportive: my employer, my manager and my work colleagues. I was the one worrying how people would take it, what I would say. How could I explain something that I didn't understand?

Importantly, the rehabilitation involved a gradual return to work. It was a well-managed process. For instance, after meeting with the personnel manager the first time, I met with both her and my line manager, again on neutral territory for coffee in an hotel. It helped just to talk about work and how to best phase me back in. With my consent, as well as obtaining general occupational health advice, my personnel manager would discuss my welfare with my consultant psychiatrist – not the detail of my illness, but the practical things to help ease me back into work. At every stage the options were also discussed and agreed with me. We talked about the job, likes, dislikes, strengths and weaknesses, but there was no pressure to change. However, at our first, brief planning meeting while I was off work, in spite of the informal conversation in restful surroundings, I was still very tense and anxious. Although I was lucid intellectually, emotionally I felt very sensitive, vulnerable.

After I had been off work for three months the rehabilitation involved being phased back in gently over

> a further three months: a few hours, a few days at a
> time to three and four days a week. Initially, I would
> arrive at work later and leave earlier. This would help
> counteract the sleepiness caused by the medication in
> the mornings and also help to avoid the usual pressures
> of rush hour.

In the case study above notice that there was deadline pressure, and that this person was not applying simple stress-management strategies such as taking a proper lunch break:

> factors included the constant pressure to meet deadlines, lunch only
> being a hurried sandwich at the desk.

In our experience as psychologists, so often our stressed clients have stopped taking lunch breaks. These are so important to help us unwind and keep work in perspective. Also it has the benefit of reducing our blood pressure as we switch off.

Notice how he started to take project feedback too personally and felt insulted, possibly putting his ego on the line (see Chapter 3):

> On one occasion, I took what most would regard as a 'minor conflict'
> with a senior manager at work (over a stress research project, no less!)
> as a major personal insult, and this blew the lid off everything for me.

His behaviour became more erratic, and fortunately his manager and his boss raised this problem with him. On their recommendation he saw his doctor, and on being admitted into psychiatric care he experienced 'an acute psychotic episode'. His employers were supportive, and his rehabilitation involved a gradual return to work.

## Activity 36
## Stressed colleagues

Think back over the past two years. Can you think of any colleagues who suffered from high levels of work-related stress who needed to take time off work? Were there any tell-tale signs or was it totally unexpected?

## How do you cope with stress at work?

The case study highlighted that employees may respond to pressures and demands at work in a manner that may exacerbate stress in themselves. It is useful to assess how you deal with work-related problems. The next activity will provide you with an insight into helpful and unhelpful methods of dealing with stress.

## Activity 37
## Coping with Work Stress Questionnaire

When you have a work-related problem or stress, to what extent do you do the following? Circle one number for each of the following statements that apply to you.

## Table 7.1

| | Never | Rarely | Periodically | Regularly | Very often |
|---|---|---|---|---|---|
| **Helpful behaviour** | | | | | |
| Seek support and advice from supervisors | 1 | 2 | 3 | 4 | 5 |
| Try to deal with the situation objectively in an unemotional way | 1 | 2 | 3 | 4 | 5 |
| Try to recognise your own limitations | 1 | 2 | 3 | 4 | 5 |
| Talk to understanding colleagues | 1 | 2 | 3 | 4 | 5 |
| Set priorities and deal with problems accordingly | 1 | 2 | 3 | 4 | 5 |
| Accept the situation and learn to live with it | 1 | 2 | 3 | 4 | 5 |
| Seek as much social support as possible | 1 | 2 | 3 | 4 | 5 |
| **Unhelpful behaviour** | | | | | |
| 'Staying busy' | 1 | 2 | 3 | 4 | 5 |
| 'Bottling things up' | 1 | 2 | 3 | 4 | 5 |
| Using distractions (to take your mind off things) | 1 | 2 | 3 | 4 | 5 |
| Smoking more | 1 | 2 | 3 | 4 | 5 |
| Delegating the problem | 1 | 2 | 3 | 4 | 5 |
| Drinking alcohol rather more than usual | 1 | 2 | 3 | 4 | 5 |
| Trying to avoid the situation | 1 | 2 | 3 | 4 | 5 |

Unhelpful                    Helpful

14                    42                    70

Source: adapted from Cooper *et al* (1988).

Total your scores and plot the total on the scale above. A score of 42 or higher is preferable. Look at your low-scoring items. What can you do to improve these low scores?

# The unfit manager

The previous activity focused on any employee. In this section we focus on managers. Psychologists Dinah Jenkins and Stephen Palmer published stress research in 2004 which highlighted two types of managers: the fit manager and the unfit manager. There were key differences in their behaviour and general attitudes and perceptions. The unfit managers suffered from most organisational pressures and demonstrated significant symptoms of stress. Their study focused on the National Health Service but is probably applicable to managers in general (Palmer, 2007b).

# Activity 38
# Are you an unfit manager?

Whether you are a manager, supervisor or in another position at work, tick the items below that apply to you. You:
- do not appear very self-aware or deny your stress-related symptoms;
- do not have a supportive relationship with your line manager;
- do not ask for help within the workplace;
- have accountability without authority (low control);
- interpret the managerial contract with the organisation literally, that is, 'work as many hours as it takes to complete the task';

- perceive your psychological contract with the organisation to be violated – promises unmet, career paths withdrawn (expectations unmet) (effort/reward imbalance);
- have too much compatibility of values and goals of commitment and vocation (over-committed);
- give more than you get in the social exchange of work (over-work);
- use emotion-focused coping as a main strategy;
- do not pay attention to your physical and mental health;
- do not set boundaries, limits or parameters on your expectations of self and your role as a manager: for instance you go until you drop, 'burn the candle at both ends' and in the middle;
- have 'boundless' optimism which drives you on with the hope of 'jam tomorrow' and rewards for your labours but which may not come to fruition (over-optimistic);
- do not set boundaries on your hours of working (over-tired);
- do not set boundaries or deny what your body and mind can cope with;
- do not engage in/make time for physical exercise or stress-relieving pastimes/rituals, although you know they are helpful;
- do not set boundaries or balance the work–home interface (over-involved with work);
- have a distorted view of a manager's professional identity and hold stereotypical expectations of managers (as a manager I should do or be able to do ...).

Now reflect on those items you have ticked. Consider how you could change these behaviours, attitudes or perceptions.

To summarise, unfit managers generally lack balance, particularly between work and home life. They may be over-committed, over-involved, over-worked and under-aware of the psychological and physical health consequences of workplace strain. Interestingly, they may be confident and have self-efficacy (belief that they can do the task), but they do not set boundaries on workload and hours of work.

## The fit manager

The fit manager has more resistance to stress than the unfit manager. Some of the key factors in staying psychologically and physically fit include a robust, people-oriented personality style, asking for help when required, and the availability and use of a trustworthy, supportive line manager. Of course, the organisation may not have a supportive culture and may lack supportive managers. However, that is the responsibility of the organisation, and could be addressed.

## Activity 39
## Are you a fit manager?

Whether you are a manager, supervisor or in another position at work, tick the items below that apply to you. You are a 'people person' who is mindful, pragmatic, optimistic and:

- has positive, well-bounded, *reciprocal relationships* with subordinates, peers, your line manager and the organisation;
- has a *robust personality* (hardiness) and *professional self-efficacy*;
- operates in a state of corporate *mindfulness*;
- practises *self-awareness* and *self-monitoring*;

- defines, delimits and protects your *boundaries* of tolerance (physically, socially, mentally);
- has a sense of *control of workload* through skilled management practices;
- is *realistic* about what you can and cannot achieve;
- has realistic expectations of the organisation (*psychological contract*) and your role as a manager (professional identity);
- proficiently accesses and utilises (internal and external) resources and support;
- maintains *flexible* attitudes and can adapt to change;
- delivers your *targets*;
- has motivation, enthusiasm, commitment, job satisfaction, and a sense of *meaning* through work;
- looks after your *body* – exercise, diet, relaxation;
- *balances* work and home life.

Importantly, these psychologically robust and healthy managers also:

- know when they need help and will *ask for support*;
- have a confidential, trusting, listening, understanding, and mutually rewarding (reciprocal) working relationship with their *line manager*.

Now reflect on those items you have not ticked. Consider how you could change these behaviours, attitudes or perceptions.

The research indicated that the healthiest manager is one who calls him- or herself a '*people person*'. He or she: values, respects and supports his or her staff and colleagues; has excellent communication skills, shares information; is sensitive to other people's moods and concerns, encourages feedback from subordinates about his/her management style and ways of working; develops, trains and supports new employees; has an open-door policy; offers a sounding board to others; is team-oriented, and believes that people are the organisation's biggest resource and best asset.

We suggest that the characteristics of the fit manager would be beneficial for many employees, and could be actively encouraged in organisations wanting to address stress at work.

# Work-related stress risk assessment and interventions

Organisational stress management and prevention programmes can have a positive impact upon employees' physical and psychological health, improve performance, lower sickness absence and reduce staff turnover. The HSE recommends that organisations undertake work-related stress (WRS) risk assessments, and manage or prevent WRS. The HSE has developed relevant management standards for six key areas of work design that, if not properly managed, are associated with poor health and well-being, lower productivity and increased sickness absence. In other words, the six management standards cover the primary sources of stress at work. These are:

- **Demands – such as workload, work patterns and the work environment.**
- **Control – such as how much say people have in the way they do their work.**
- **Support – such as the encouragement, sponsorship and resources provided by the organisation, line management and colleagues.**
- **Relationships – such as promoting positive working to avoid conflict, and dealing with unacceptable behaviour such as bullying.**
- **Role – such as whether people understand their role within the organisation and whether the organisation ensures that they do not have conflicting roles.**

- Change – such as how organisational change (large or small) is managed and communicated in the organisation.

Employers have a duty to ensure that risks arising from work activity are properly controlled. The management standards approach helps employers work with their employees and representatives to undertake risk assessments for stress.

The relationship between these hazards, the symptoms of stress for the employee or organisation, and the negative outcomes is illustrated in the model of work stress in Figure 7.1.

# Activity 40
# Assessing potential hazards

The key questions developed by the HSE that you can ask yourself or your colleagues regarding these potential hazards are listed below. Those marked (N) are negative and those marked (P) are positive. Mark the items that apply to you.

## Demands

- Different groups at work demand things from me that are hard to combine (N)
- I have unachievable deadlines (N)
- I have to work very intensively (N)
- I have to neglect some tasks because I have too much to do (N)
- I am unable to take sufficient breaks (N)
- I am pressured to work long hours (N)
- I have to work very fast (N)
- I have unrealistic time pressures (N)

# Model of Work Stress

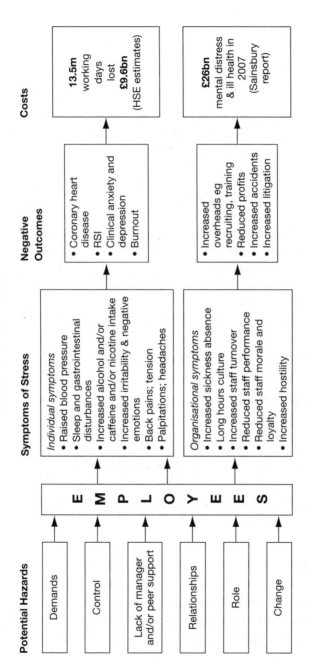

Source: adapted from Palmer, Cooper and Thomas (2001).

**Figure 7.1** A model of work stress

## Control

- I can decide when to take a break (P)
- I have a say in my own work speed (P)
- I have a choice in deciding how I do my work (P)
- I have a choice in deciding what I do at work (P)
- I have some say over the way I work (P)
- My working time can be flexible (P)

## Manager's support

- I am given supportive feedback on the work I do (P)
- I can rely on my line manager to help me out with a work problem (P)
- I can talk to my line manager about something that has upset or annoyed me about work (P)
- I am supported through emotionally demanding work (P)
- My line manager encourages me at work (P)

## Peer support

- If work gets difficult, my colleagues will help me (P)
- I get help and support I need from colleagues (P)
- I receive the respect at work I deserve from my colleagues (P)
- My colleagues are willing to listen to my work-related problems (P)

## Role

- I am clear what is expected of me at work (P)
- I know how to go about getting my job done (P)
- I am clear what my duties and responsibilities are (P)

- I am clear about the goals and objectives for my department (P)
- I understand how my work fits into the overall aim of the organisation (P)

## Change

- I have sufficient opportunities to question managers about change at work (P)
- Staff are always consulted about change at work (P)
- When changes are made at work, I am clear how they will work out in practice (P)

You have just undertaken a rough and ready mini-stress audit. Look at the items you marked (N). If they occur on a regular basis, you and/or your employer may need to address these items. Also consider the (P) items that did not apply to you. Again these may be areas you or your employer may need or wish to address.

You can find out more about the HSE Management Standards indicator, which includes rating scales from never to always, and how it can be used in your organisation on the HSE website:

www.hse.gov.uk/stress/standards/downloads.htm

The HSE website includes a free analysis tool and other useful documents to assist in its use.

# Before you start a work-stress risk assessment

Initially it is important to secure management commitment especially from senior managers. Three issues that can be discussed at this stage are (HSE, 2009):

## 1 The legal case

Many countries will have specific laws relating to tackling stress and/or more general laws that encompass stress and mental health under health and safety legislation.

## 2 The business case: tackling stress brings business benefits

Work-related stress has been shown to have adverse effects for organisations in terms of:

- employee commitment to work;
- staff performance and productivity;
- staff turnover and intention to leave;
- attendance levels;
- staff recruitment and retention;
- customer satisfaction;
- organisational image and reputation;
- potential litigation.

## 3 The moral/ethical case: tackling stress prevents ill-health

It has been found that prolonged periods of stress can lead to both physical illnesses – such as heart disease, back pain – and psychological disorders – such as anxiety, phobias and depression. In addition it can trigger unhealthy behaviours leading to ill-health such as increased smoking, comfort-eating snack food and consuming more alcohol and caffeinated drinks.

At this initial stage it is advisable to set up a steering group involving key stakeholders such as employees, Trade Union representatives, occupational health and safety officers, and so on. The steering group could develop a project plan, secure adequate resources including staff availability, and develop a communications strategy in order to engage employees in the stress-prevention programme. If appropriate, the steering group or other key representatives could develop a stress policy for the organisation (see Appendix). The stress policy could be viewed as a work in progress as the steering group may revise it later once the stress-prevention programme is being undertaken and feedback is obtained from staff.

The HSE recommends that employers should undertake a five-step risk assessment to assess the work-related stress hazards. This process is described below:

## Step 1: Identify the risk factors

Members of the steering group and other key people involved in the stress-prevention programme need to become knowledgeable about the HSE Management Standards and their relevance to their organisation. The standards relate to:

- Factor 1: Demands
- Factor 2: Control
- Factor 3: Support – (Manager's and Peer)
- Factor 4: Relationships
- Factor 5: Role
- Factor 6: Change.

It is important to understand how to compare your company's performance with the good management practice, focusing on addressing the real organisational causes of work-related stress, such as work overload, instead of just considering the time-management training option.

# Step 2: Decide who might be harmed and how

The HSE emphasises that any employee regardless of age, gender, status, ethnicity or disability, can suffer from stress. Particular staff may be at higher risk at different times for work or personal reasons; for example, divorce, pregnancy, a recent bereavement, working away from home or family illness.

There are a variety of methods to obtain relevant data. Both qualitative and quantitative data-gathering methods could be used, for example:

- *QUALITATIVE:* Focus groups; performance appraisal; informal discussions with staff; return-to-work interviews; exit interviews.
- *QUANTITATIVE:* Productivity and performance data; absence/sickness data; Employee Assistance Programmes (EAPs) data; staff turnover; questionnaires; stress audits; HSE work-related stress tool.

Surveys and questionnaires such as the HSE Management Standards Indicator Tool can be used (see page 154) and the results compared to the Management Standards. In our experience it is easier to use the freely available Excel-based analysis tool than the paper version as it instantly provides the comparison between your organisation and the Management Standards. The tool can be used in conjunction with other in-house surveys or instruments. Commercially available tools can be used instead although there is usually a fee.

When collecting data it is important that personal information is kept anonymous and confidential, otherwise employees will not wish to complete work-stress questionnaires.

Surveys are only the first part of a work-related stress risk assessment so care should be given when providing feedback to the organisation and employees about any preliminary findings.

## Step 3: Evaluate the risk: explore problems and develop solutions

By this step, the steering group probably has a lot of data from surveys and other sources. In our experience it can be somewhat overwhelming unless it is broken down and dealt with systematically. At this stage how hazards could negatively affect the department/unit/division are considered.

Questions to reflect upon include:

- **What action is already being taken?**
- **Is it enough?**
- **What more is required?**
- **Who needs to either action it or do it?**

It is important at this step to communicate the results and provide feedback to employees, management and other representatives; dealing with any individual concerns raised. Instead of just focusing on the problems it is crucial to start developing solutions. Employees can be actively engaged through the use of focus groups to discuss the issues and seek solutions.

Whenever possible, the focus is on the elimination of risks or hazards at an organisational level. This is considered more important than just offering employees stress-management training or stress counselling. However, in many cases a comprehensive programme including health promotion, coaching, training and counselling helps both the organisation and employees.

## Step 4: Record your findings: develop and implement action plans

In the UK, organisations that employ five or more employees must record the main findings of the risk assessment. A summary of the report should be available for employees. To maintain confidentiality, employees should not be identifiable from the report. This document can be used to monitor progress, especially in dealing with particular work-related stress hazards. Although there is no set format for an action plan the HSE provides a template and an example of how it can be completed (see Tables 7.2 and 7.3).

## Step 5: Monitor and review: monitor and review action plans and assess effectiveness

The risk assessment should be reviewed whenever significant changes occur in the department or organisation. This would include the method by which a department handles its day-to-day business. This review would be in consultation with employees. It is recommended that the assessment be reviewed on a regular basis. It is important to check whether the solutions are tackling the problems effectively and ensure that review meetings are being held.

# A comprehensive approach

A comprehensive stress-prevention programme would include primary, secondary and tertiary interventions:

- **Primary: Remove the hazards or reduce employees' exposure to/impact upon them.**
- **Secondary: Improve the organisation's ability to recognise and deal with stress-related problems.**
- **Tertiary: Help employees cope with and recover from problems at work.**

Primary interventions include undertaking stress audits or work-related stress assessments, and eliminating the hazards. Secondary interventions can include training managers and supervisors to recognise stress in their staff, and to learn how to intervene at both the organisational and individual levels.

**Table 7.2**

**Health and Safety Executive    Management Standards for Tackling Work Related Stress**

**Action plan template**

| Standard area | Desired state | Current state | Practical solutions | Who will take the work forward? | When? | How will staff receive feedback? | Action completed? |
|---|---|---|---|---|---|---|---|
| | | | | | | | |

**Table 7.3**

**Health and Safety Executive      Management Standards for Tackling Work Related Stress**

**Action plan template**

| Demands | Desired state | Current state | Practical solutions | Who will take the work forward | When? | How will staff receive feedback? | Action completed? |
|---|---|---|---|---|---|---|---|
| | *Average to good performance* | *Bad/very bad performance* | | | | | |
| The organisation provides employees with adequate and achievable demands in relation to the agreed hours of work | | Workloads are not planned and peaks often occur during summer when people are on annual leave | 1. Plan the work better and if peaks do clash with fixed annual leave commitments consider talking to other departments to see if temporary resources can be provided | 1. Line managers to lead and suggest the idea to senior managers | Issue to be raised at next senior managers meeting | 1. Via monthly meetings, staff bulletins | Yes. [Date] |
| | | | 2. Employees to talk to line managers about upcoming leave and potential difficulties with workload during monthly meetings | 2. All, with line manager to lead | Immediately | 2. During monthly meetings | Yes – activity ongoing |

Teaching managers coaching skills that they can use with staff may help to improve performance and thereby reduce stress. If a manager realises that an employee is stressed, a tertiary-level intervention could include referral to the Employee Assistance Programme or a stress counselling service. This would not exclude a parallel primary-level intervention such as dealing with the long-hours culture or unrealistic work demands.

## What can you do?

If you believe that there are high levels of stress at work that are not being dealt with, you may wish to encourage your employers to take the matter more seriously. We list below a number of interventions that you could consider making.

- **Check whether colleagues agree with your point of view. Discuss the issue of stress with them. Perhaps show them the list of individual symptoms (pages 33–35) and the list of organisational hazards and stressors (pages 141–142).**
- **Investigate whether your organisation already has a stress policy.**
- **If you and your colleagues do feel that stress exists, consider discussing this issue with your supervisor, manager or director, or with a representative from occupational health, training, human resources/ personnel or the appropriate trade union.**
- **Set up a working party of colleagues interested in assessing levels of stress and in developing (if needed) a stress management programme.**
- **Consider in what ways your organisational culture contributes to stress.**
- **Undertake a stress audit to discover the levels of stress. Use a professional consultancy or suitably qualified colleagues in-house (see the list of useful organisations**

at the back of the book). Consider how to manage the important issue of confidentiality with regard to stress questionnaires. If staff do not believe that their individual answers will remain confidential, they are less likely to complete the questionnaire.

- Stress management or managing pressure workshops or courses can help employees (see pages 191 and 192 for providers). In addition, a focus on dealing with the causes of stress at work, such as a long-hours culture or aggressive managers, may be beneficial.

## Summary

- Both excessive external pressures and self-induced internal pressures we place upon ourselves can trigger stress.
- Managers can be fit or unfit in terms of how they approach their work and communicate with others.
- To address stress, performance and well-being at work the HSE has developed six key management standards that employers can strive for.
- There are six key potential causes of stress at work: demands, control, a lack of managers' and peer support, relationships, role and change.
- Work-related stress risk assessment provides the employer with a clearer picture of the sources of stress that need to be tackled.
- The development of a company stress policy is a good starting point (see Appendix).

Now make notes on what you have learnt.

# Stress self-audit

Before we move on to the last chapter, in which you will develop your own stress management action plan, it will be useful to review key stress questionnaires you have previously completed. This will help you to learn more about yourself and how to reduce your stress levels.

Go back through the book and note down below the scores you obtained for the following questionnaires:

**Table 8.1**

| Questionnaire | Score |
|---|---|
| Personality and behavioural variables | |
| Type A, Type B (pages 102–103) | _____ |
| Locus of control (pages 18–20) | _____ |
| Life event scored (pages 29–32) | _____ |
| Stress moderators | |
| Social support, personal problems (page 105) | _____ |
| Social support, work problems (page 106) | _____ |
| Coping with life stress (pages 15–16) | _____ |
| Coping with work stress (pages 147–148) | _____ |

Plot your scores below and join up consecutive points:

## Table 8.2

**Personality and behavioural variables**

| Type B | 14 | 84 | 154 | Type A |
|---|---|---|---|---|
| Internal locus of control | 10 | 30 | 50 | External locus of control |
| Life event scored | I | 50 | 100 | |

**Stress moderators**

| Social support personal problems | 0 | 10 | 40 | |
|---|---|---|---|---|
| | low | | high | |
| Social support work problems | 0 | 10 | 50 | |
| Coping with life stress | 29 | 87 | 145 | |
| Coping with work stress | 14 | 42 | 70 | |

Now compare your profile with the four examples below. We have provided examples ranging from low to high vulnerability to stress. Does your profile look similar to one of those illustrated?

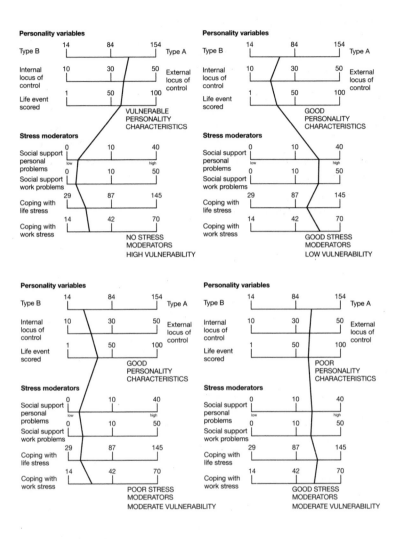

Source: Cooper *et al* (1988).

**Figure 8.1**   Stress profile examples

Look at the scores. You are now in a position to reduce stress by changing your scores in the different areas relating to stress. For example, if you have a high locus of control score, consider how you could modify your beliefs to reduce the score. If you have a low coping with life stress score, consider what you could do to increase it. Do this for all the questionnaires, and consider what strategies and techniques you could use to help you change.

These changes can form part of your action plan, which you can develop in the next chapter. It is useful to rescore the questionnaires every three months to see how you are progressing.

Now make notes on this chapter.

# 9

# Developing your own action plan

Now that you have (we hope) read all the previous chapters and undertaken some of the activity exercises, you will be in a position to develop your own action plan. Therefore you are only a few steps away from becoming a 'life manager'. However, there are a few loose ends to tie up before we arrive at the action plan, and we shall now focus on them.

## 'Stress carriers'

When you are under pressure at home or at work, how do you react? Do you:

- **rush around like a headless chicken?**
- **become irritable?**
- **bang tables or desks with your fist?**
- **become aggressive?**
- **stop making pleasantries with family and colleagues?**
- **sulk or withdraw?**

- **blame others?**
- **shout at yourself or others?**
- **become cynical or sarcastic?**
- **deny reality?**
- **'awfulise' about the possible outcome?**
- **start bullying others?**

If you do any of the above, what is likely to be the effect on your friends, colleagues, partner or family? Do they become more helpful or less so? Do you motivate or demotivate others? Does your behaviour help you to achieve your goals, whatever they are, when you are under pressure?

In our experience, people exhibiting a number of the above behaviours tend to be a trigger of stress in others around them, which leads to greater stress or inefficiency (or both) within a team or family. In recent years people like this have been called 'stress carriers', owing to their negative effect upon others close at hand. In extreme cases they may not notice any effect on themselves and sadly be unaware of their impact upon others. Similar to Typhoid Mary, who did not succumb to the effects of typhoid yet infected many of her customers, stress carriers often inflict stress upon anybody they come into contact with, but themselves survive (in the short term) remarkably unscathed.

If you believe that you have a tendency to be a stress carrier, you may wish to consider which behaviours you should target for action.

# Home–work interface

In our experience, people who are encountering occupational stress are unlikely just to leave it at work. It usually has an effect on their personal life, because they are unable to switch off their problems on arriving home. They do not necessarily kick the cat as they return from work, but they may be irritable and angry, or just withdraw into themselves and prefer the television for company. Likewise, if partners are having relationship difficulties or sleepless nights because their baby keeps them awake, this can adversely affect their work life. Either way, the home–work interface often needs to be managed carefully to ensure that there is little or no overspill from one to the other. Strategies discussed in earlier chapters may need to be applied, such as thinking skills, imagery and relaxation exercises, and assertiveness skills.

## Action plan

When you are going to go shopping you probably make a list of what you wish to purchase. If you are organising a wedding or managing a project, then you are again very likely to plan goals and targets. Developing your own conquering stress action plan is no different.

## Activity 41
## Reviewing the activities

**Look back through the previous chapters at the activity exercises. Note down any areas that relate to your general thinking skills or skills deficits, imagery skills, behaviour or physical health that you believe need further development to help you conquer stress. Reviewing the results of the self-assessment questionnaires may help this process. Review also the notes you may have made at the end of each chapter.**

After completing Activity 41 you will have a list of areas that you may wish to work on to help you to deal with or prevent stress. The next stage is to write up your action plan. A helpful strategy is to break down the process into the three key areas: psychological (thinking and imagery), behavioural and health. To help you we include here a sample plan. The action plan can be revised and updated as and when necessary.

# Sample stress management action plan

Action to be taken by: Jayne                    Date: 28 February

## 1 Psychological

### Thinking skills

Stop making mountains out of molehills! Keep events in perspective: life's a hassle but seldom a horror!

Quit holding on to rigid, demanding 'musts' and 'shoulds'. This will reduce the pressure upon me, my family and staff.

Remember that I am not my behaviour! If I fail at some task, it does not mean that I'm a total failure.

### Imagery skills

If life gets on top of me, use time projection imagery to remind myself that in a few months' time the situation won't seem so bad.

## 2 Behavioural

### Social support

Make an effort to cultivate more colleagues at work. Have a few more non-work-related chats with people. This needn't take up much extra time. I'll start taking tea breaks and chat then.

Start regularly going out to the cinema again with my partner. Ensure we go out with friends at least once a month.

### Assertiveness

Practise saying no. Start thinking of the consequences of

taking on additional work before answering positively to my colleagues' requests.

Make a big effort to reduce my whinging to my colleagues and partner, and stop blaming others so often.

### Time management
Avoid procrastinating! Remind myself that my boss only wants a good job done and not 110 per cent. I elevate tasks into burdens with my thinking errors.

## 3 Physical health

### Exercise
Incorporate exercise into my daily routine: three days a week I'll walk to work; at least once a day I'll use the stairs at work and not the lift; I'll take up badminton again and play at weekends.

### Nutrition
I'll eat red meat once a week only. I'll attempt to eat fish three times a week.

If I fancy a snack, I'll eat some fruit.

I'll give semi-skimmed milk a go for two weeks. If I get used to the taste then I'll continue. I'll drink less coffee and more tea instead.

### Relaxation
Before bedtime I'll spend 10 minutes using relaxation imagery. At work I'll 'make' the opportunity to use relaxation imagery just before I go home to help me switch off and leave my work stresses where they belong – at work.

# Activity 42
# Stress management action plan

**Now complete your stress management action plan. Once**

you have developed your action plan – that is, once you have finished this activity – you will be on the path to becoming a 'stress manager'. You may find it useful to use a PC or laptop to record your action plan.

## Stress management action plan

Action to be taken by:                    Date:

1 Psychological

2 Behavioural

3 Physical health

You will not have quite finished, because you could also become a 'life manager' who plans ahead and does not leave important issues to chance. This is the last activity in this book.

# Activity 43
# The future

Have you thought about your future? Think about how you might deal with any of the following life events that may conceivably apply to you:

- partner leaves you;
- partner becomes seriously ill or dies;
- birth of a child or children;
- child or children start school;
- child or children finish school;
- adult child leaves home;
- you receive promotion or demotion;
- losing or changing jobs;

- **long-term unemployment;**
- **physical disability or illness;**
- **encountering sexual difficulties;**
- **change in residence.**

Life managers spend a few minutes every month thinking about how to deal with a range of difficult issues. They may update their CV every three months and decide whether they need more training or need to move into a new area of work. If problems crop up at work, they are already prepared for action. On retirement, they are unlikely to retire to the country or a dormitory seaside town without first ensuring that they know the place well, perhaps even spending many weekends there over a period of years in order to develop a support network of friends before deciding to make the final move. Perhaps they have purchased a second home there 10 years earlier – a good investment, too.

Although children are very important to them, life manager couples will have ensured that they have maintained a good relationship with each other and put aside time for themselves, so that when the children finally leave home they do not experience an overwhelming sense of loss and do not need to overhaul their relationship.

## Start now

Reading a book on successful stress management is the easy part. Armchair stress experts exist all over the world. We often meet them! Use the motivation imagery exercise on pages 94–95 and think of the benefits to you, your family and colleagues. The best way to master stress and become more resilient is to start now and not leave it to chance. You can do it!

## Summary

- **Stress carriers create stress for others.**
- **A stress management action plan helps you to maintain focus on your goals.**

Now make notes on what you have learnt.

# Appendix

## An example of a stress policy
### Introduction

We are committed to protecting the health, safety and welfare of our employees. We recognise that workplace stress is a health and safety issue and acknowledge the importance of identifying and reducing workplace stressors.

This policy will apply to everyone in the company. Managers are responsible for implementation and the company is responsible for providing the necessary resources.

### Definition of stress

The Health and Safety Executive defines stress as 'the adverse reaction people have to excessive pressure or other types of demand placed on them'. This makes an important distinction between pressure, which can be a positive state if managed correctly, and stress, which can be detrimental to health.

## Policy

- The company will identify all workplace stressors and conduct risk assessments to eliminate stress or control the risks from stress. These risk assessments will be regularly reviewed.
- The company will consult with Trade Union Safety Representatives on all proposed action relating to the prevention of workplace stress.
- The company will provide training for all managers and supervisory staff in good management practices.
- The company will provide confidential counselling for staff affected by stress caused by either work or external factors.
- The company will provide adequate resources to enable managers to implement the company's agreed stress management strategy.

# Responsibilities

## Managers

- Conduct and implement recommendations of risk assessments within their jurisdiction.
- Ensure good communication between management and staff, particularly where there are organisational and procedural changes.
- Ensure staff are fully trained to discharge their duties.
- Ensure staff are provided with meaningful developmental opportunities.
- Monitor workloads to ensure that people are not overloaded.
- Monitor working hours and overtime to ensure that staff are not overworking.

- Monitor holidays to ensure that staff are taking their full entitlement.
- Attend training as requested in good management practice and health and safety.
- Ensure that bullying and harassment is not tolerated within their jurisdiction.
- Be vigilant and offer additional support to a member of staff who is experiencing stress outside work, eg bereavement or separation.

## Occupational health and safety staff

- Provide specialist advice and awareness training on stress.
- Train and support managers in implementing stress risk assessments.
- Support individuals who have been off sick with stress and advise them and their management on a planned return to work.
- Refer to workplace counsellors or specialist agencies as required.
- Monitor and review the effectiveness of measures to reduce stress.
- Inform the employer and the health and safety committee of any changes and developments in the field of stress at work.

## Human resources

- Give guidance to managers on the stress policy.
- Help monitor the effectiveness of measures to address stress by collating sickness absence statistics.
- Advise managers and individuals on training requirements.

- Provide continuing support to managers and individuals in a changing environment and encourage referral to occupational workplace counsellors where appropriate.

## Employees

- Raise issues of concern with your Safety Representative, line manager or occupational health.
- Accept opportunities for counselling when recommended.

## Safety Representatives

- Safety Representatives must be meaningfully consulted on any changes to work practices or work design that could precipitate stress.
- Safety Representatives must be able to consult with members on the issue of stress including conducting any workplace surveys.
- Safety Representatives must be meaningfully involved in the risk assessment process.
- Safety Representatives should be allowed access to collective and anonymous data from HR.
- Safety Representatives should be provided with paid time away from normal duties to attend any Trade Union training relating to workplace stress.
- Safety Representatives should conduct joint inspections of the workplace at least every three months to ensure that environmental stressors are properly controlled.

## Safety Committee

- The joint Safety Committee will perform a pivotal role in ensuring that this policy is implemented.

- The Safety Committee will oversee monitoring of the efficacy of the policy and other measures to reduce stress and promote workplace health and safety.

Signed by

Managing Director:  _____

Date:  _____

Employee Representative:  _____

Date:  _____

# References and bibliography

Benson, H (1976) *The Relaxation Response*, Collins, London

Bonanno, G A (2004) Loss, trauma, and human resilience: have we underestimated the human capacity to thrive after extremely aversive events? *American Psychologist*, **59** (1), pp 20–28

Clarke, D and Palmer, S (1994) *Stress Management Trainer's Guide*, National Extension College, Cambridge

CMHA (2009) *Desjardins Financial Security Health Survey*, published in association with the Canadian Mental Health Association, Ottawa, Canada

Cooper, C L and Palmer, S (2000) *Conquer Your Stress*, CIPD, London

Cooper, C L, Cooper, R D and Eaker, L H (1988) *Living with Stress*, Penguin, Harmondsworth

Ellis, A, Gordon, J, Neenan, M and Palmer, S (1998) *Stress Counseling: A rational emotive behaviour approach*, Springer, New York

Epictetus (1890) *The Collected Works of Epictetus*, Little, Brown, Boston, Mass

Harvey, K, Kemps, E and Tiggemann, M (2005) The nature of imagery processes underying food cravings, *British Journal of Health Psychology*, **10** (1), pp 49–56

Health and Safety Executive (HSE) (2001) *Tackling Work-Related Stress: A managers' guide to improving and maintaining employee health and well-being*, HSE, Suffolk

HSE (2006a) *Rehabilitation after an Acute Episode of Work-Related Stress: A case study by an anonymous civil servant* [Online] www.hse.gov.uk/stress/rehabilitation.pdf (accessed 24 October 2006)

HSE (2006b) *Stress, Mental Health and Rehabilitation – One Man's Story* [Online] www.hse.gov.uk/stress (accessed 24 October 2006)

HSE (2006c) *Management Standards for Stress* [Online] www.hse. gov.uk/stress/standards/index.htm (accessed 24 August 2009)

International Labour Organization (ILO) (2000) *Mental Health in the Workplace*, ILO, Geneva

Jenkins, D and Palmer, S (2004) Job stress in National Health Service managers: a qualitative exploration of the stressor–strain–health relationship. The 'fit' and 'unfit' manager, *International Journal of Health Promotion and Education*, **42** (2), pp 48–63

Locke, E A (1996) Motivation through conscious goal setting, *Applied and Preventive Psychology* **5**, pp 117–124

Locke, E A and Latham, GP (1990) *A Theory of Goal Setting and Task Peformance*, Prentice Hall, Englewood Cliffs, NJ

Palmer, S (1990) Assertion, *Journal for Women in the GMB*, Northern Region

Palmer, S (1993) *Multimodal Techniques: Relaxation and hypnosis*, Centre for Stress Management and Centre for Multimodal Therapy, London

Palmer, S (1997) Self-acceptance: concept, techniques and interventions, *The Rational Emotive Behaviour Therapist*, **5** (1), pp 4–30

Palmer, S (1999) The negative travel beliefs questionnaire (NTBQ), *The Rational Emotive Behaviour Therapist*, **7** (1), pp 48–51

Palmer, S (2007a) Cognitive Coaching in the Business World. Inaugural lecture given at the Swedish Centre for Work Based Learning, Gotenbug, Sweden, 8 February

Palmer, S (2007b) Stress, performance, resilience and well-being: the 'fit' vs 'unfit' manager. Paper given at the Institute of Safety and Health National Conference, Telford, UK, 27 April

Palmer, S (2009) Inference chaining: a rational coaching technique, *Coaching Psychology International*, **2** (1), pp 11–12

Palmer, S and Burton, T (1996) *Dealing with People Problems at Work*, McGraw-Hill, Maidenhead

Palmer, S and Dryden, W (1995) *Counselling for Stress Problems*, Sage, London

Palmer, S and Neenan, M (1998) Double imagery procedure, *The Rational Emotive Behaviour Therapist*, **6** (2), pp 89–92

Palmer, S and Puri, A (2006) *Coping with Stress at University: A survival guide*, Sage, London

Palmer, S and Strickland, L (1996) *Stress Management: A quick guide*, Folens, Dunstable

Palmer, S and Wilding, C (2006) *Moody to Mellow*, Hodder Arnold, London

Palmer, S, Cooper, C and Thomas, K (2001) Model of organisational stress for use within an occupational health education/promotion or wellbeing programme – a short communication, *Health Education Journal*, **60** (4), pp 378–80

Palmer, S, Cooper, C and Thomas, K (2003a) Revised model of organisational stress for use within stress prevention/ management and wellbeing programmes, *International Journal of Health Promotion and Education*, **41**, pp 57–58

Palmer, S, Cooper, C and Thomas, K (2003b) *Creating a Balance: Managing stress*, British Library, London

Parrott, A (1991) Social drugs: their effects upon health, in M Pitts and K Phillips (eds) *The Psychology of Health: An introduction*, Routledge, London

Rotter, J B (1966) Generalised expectancies for internal versus external control of reinforcement, *Psychology Monographs: General and Applied*, **80**, pp 1–26

Ruiz-Bueno, J (2000) Locus of control, perceived control, and learned helplessness, in V Hill Rice (ed), *Handbook of Stress, Coping, and Health: Implications for nursing research, theory, and practice*, Sage, Thousand Oaks

Stansfeld, S, Head, J and Marmot M (2000) *Work Related Factors and Ill Health, Whitehall II Study*, HSE, Suffolk

Wilding, C and Palmer, S (2006) *Zero to Hero*, Hodder Arnold, London

# Useful organisations

**Alcohol Concern**
Waterbridge House, 32–36 Loman Street, London, UK
Helpline: +44 (0) 20 7922 8667 (Lines open Mon–Fri 1–5pm)
E-mail: contact@alcoholconcern.org.uk
Website: www.alcoholconcern.org.uk
Provides information, guidance and advice for those worried
about their own, or somebody else's drinking habits.

**Alcoholics Anonymous**
PO Box 1, Stonebow House, Stonebow, York YO1 7NJ, UK
Helpline: +44 (0)845 769 7555 (24-hour service)
E-mail: aanewcomer@runbox.com
Website: www.alcoholics-anonymous.org.uk

**American Academy of Experts in Traumatic Stress**
368 Veterans Memorial Highway, Commack NY 11725, USA
Tel: +1 516 543 2217
Website: www.aaets.org

Holds an international register of experts in stress management, traumatic stress and bereavement, also publishes useful material on trauma.

**Association for Coaching**
66 Church Road, London W7 1LB, UK
Website: www.associationforcoaching.com

Provides a register of coaches.

**Association for Rational Emotive Behaviour Therapy**
Englewood, Farningham Hill Road, Farningham, Kent DA4 0JR, UK
Website: www.arebt.org

Holds a register of accredited therapists, counsellors and coaches.

**British Association for Behavioural and Cognitive Psychotherapies**
PO Box 9, Accrington BB5 2GD, UK
Telephone: +44 (0) 1254 875277
Website: www.babcp.org.uk

Provides a list of accredited cognitive-behavioural and rational-emotive therapists. These approaches focus on a person's unhelpful thinking and behaviours, which is similar to the approach advocated by this book.

**British Association for Counselling and Psychotherapy**
BACP House, 15 St John's Business Park, Lutterworth LE17 4HB, UK
Tel: 0870 443 5252
Website: www.bacp.co.uk

Provides a list of accredited counsellors and relevant organisations.

**British Nutrition Foundation**
High Holburn House, 52–54 High Holburn, London WC1V 6RQ, UK
Telephone: +44 (0) 20 7404 6504
Website: www.nutrition.org.uk

**British Psychological Society**
St Andrews House, 48 Princes Road East, Leicester LE1 7DR, UK
Telephone: +44 (0) 116 254 9568
Website: www.bps.org.uk

Holds a register of chartered psychologists.

**Centre for Stress Management & Centre for Coaching**
156 Westcombe Hill, London SE3 7DH, UK
Telephone: +44 (0) 20 8318 4448
Website: www.managingstress.com
Website: www.centreforcoaching.com

Provides stress counselling, coaching and training services, and undertakes stress audits and interventions at work. Has mail-order service of relevant stress management and health-related books. Runs distance learning programmes and stress management courses using the approach advocated in this book.

**Chartered Institute of Personnel and Development**
151 The Broadway, London SW19 1JQ, UK
Telephone: +44 (0) 20 8971 9000
Website: www.cipd.co.uk

Professional body that publishes a range of useful books and materials.

**Eating Disorders Association**
1st Floor, Wensum House, 103 Prince of Wales Road, Norwich NR1 1DW, UK
National Helpline: +44 (0)845 634 1414
Helpline e-mail: helpmail@edauk.com
Website: www.edauk.com

A charity providing information, help and support for people affected by eating disorders.

**General Hypnotherapy Register**
PO Box 204, Lymington SO41 6WP, UK
Tel/Fax: +44 (0)1590 683770
Website: www.general-hypnotherapy-register.com/

A national UK register of hypnotherapists.

**International Stress Management Association**
PO Box 348, Waltham Cross EN8 8XL, UK
Telephone: +44 (0) 7000 780430
Website: www.isma.org.uk

Provides information about stress management and accredits stress trainers.

**Relate**
Relationships hotline: +44 (0) 845 130 4010
Website: www.relate.org.uk

A provider of relationship counselling and sex therapy.

**Robertson Cooper Ltd**
Williams House, Manchester Science Park, Lloyd Street North
Manchester M15 6SE, UK
Tel: +44 (0)870 3333 591
Fax: +44 (0)870 3333 592

Stress audits/consultancy and applied research.

**The Samaritans**
The Upper Mill, Kingston Road, Ewell, Surrey KT17 2AF, UK
If you are in crisis you can write to the Samaritans: Chris,
PO Box 90, Stirling FK8 2SA, UK

Use this web address to locate the closest Samaritans branch to you: www.samaritans.org.uk/talk/local_branch.shtm
Tel: +44 (0) 8457 90 90 90 (open 24 hours a day)
E-mail: Jo@samaritans.org

**Society for Coaching Psychology**
Website: www.societyforcoachingpsychology.net

Holds a register for accredited coaching psychologists.

**United Kingdom Council for Psychotherapy**
2nd Floor, Edward House, 2 Wakley Street, London EC1V 7LT, UK
Tel: +44 (0) 20 7014 9955
Fax: +44 (0) 20 7014 9977
E-mail: info@psychotherapy.org.uk
Website: www.psychotherapy.org.uk

Holds a register of psychotherapists.

# Creating Success series

The above titles are available from all good bookshops.
For further information on these and other Kogan Page titles, or
to order online, visit the Kogan Page website at
**www.koganpage.com**

With over 1,000 titles in printed and digital format, **Kogan Page** offers affordable, sound business advice

**www.koganpage.com**